What Steinbeck Left Out

Pseudo Sins & Other Observations

PHIL BOWHAY

What Steinbeck Left Out

Pseudo Sins & Other Observations

PHIL BOWHAY

First Edition July 2011

© 2011 Phil Bowhay

ISBN: 978-1-935530-45-9

Printed in the U.S.A.

Published by
Park Place Publications
P.O. Box 829
Pacific Grove, CA 93950
www.parkplacepublications.com

For additional copies, e-mail: pbowhay@aol.com

What Steinbeck Left Out

Pseudo Sins & Other Observations

Table of Contents

Introduction	*vii*
How Dry I Was!	1
Give Gophers a Name	3
How Now	5
Tell Me About High School	7
Teachers	9
Bully Beware!	11
How to Build a Fire	13
Halloween!	15
Hair	17
Happy Birthday, etc.	19
R.I.P.	21
Speak to Me!	23
Going Up!	26
The High Cost of Cleanliness!	28
Books!	30
Double Your Pleasure	32
Lovely Old Ladies	34
As the Days Dwindle Down	37
Resolutions	39
Bent Twig	41
Felice Cumpleaños	43
Are We There Yet?	45
The Old Kit Bag, Revisited	47
Dress Right!	49
Easy Virtue, but Virtue Still	51
Missing The Boat!	53
Journalism 101	55

At Your Service! 57

For The Bible Tells Me So! 59

Get Out The Vote, or Just Get Out! 61

Good Old Golden Rule Days! 63

Good Scents! 65

PG Food... Before Julia! 67

Down to the Sea Again! 69

Waltz Me Around Again, Willie! 71

Music! 73

How to Save Pacific Grove! (maybe) 75

I Love a Parade! 76

Articles of Lasting Interest 78

Innocence 80

Forbidden Fruit 82

Button Up Your Overcoat! 84

Letters 86

The *Real* Fishermen's Wharves 88

No Friend Like An Old Friend 90

Open Wide! 92

Home Base 94

Among My Souvenirs 96

Out Of The Mud 98

Turn The Radio On! 100

Over Easy! 103

A Spoonful of Sugar 105

Resolve!!! 107

Roughing It! 108

Yearbook Archives 110

Confessions of a Shoe Dog 112

Everybody's Born Barefoot 115

More Library! 117

Thank You, Western Union 119

Gold! 121

Car Sick! 123

Tilt! 124

To Look Sharp! 126

Just Before Dawn! 128

Early Housekeeping 130

Yeah, Yeah, Yeah! 132

Paint! 134

Thanks a Lot! 136

Time Sensitive 138

Ballet! Not Belly! 140

Semper Fry! 142

Sea Fever 144

Good-bye Gertie 146

Defining Moments... 148

Drive-Ins! 150

Crowning Glory 152

Some Books Smell Better Than Others 154

The Power of No! 156

Praise the Aged! 158

Pacific Grove, by Golly! 160

Pre-Judge... or Prejudice 162

Sing Along With Me 164

Cool, Clear Water 166

Introduction

OK, Friends! If you missed any of my Flashback columns in *The Monterey County Herald* in the last three years, you're in luck! Here they are, with a few additions. I deeply appreciate the encouragement, inspiration, memories and suggestions from you locals. My kids and my sweetie have been the most discerning critics, approving of every single word!

Patricia Hamilton of Park Place Publications deserves the Patience Prize, along with my gratitude.

A special thanks to the best newspaper in California, *The Monterey County Herald*, with forever thanks to that great editor, Royal Calkins, an honest-to-goodness, real newspaper man! Perfect at light sanding and an occasional nudge!

Just so you will feel better about buying this book – great for gifts – proceeds from the first 500 copies to my hometown library, in Pacific Grove!

What Steinbeck Left Out

Pseudo Sins & Other Observations

How Dry I Was!

"Lips that touch wine will never touch mine!" said Mom, and it was a very good thing that my dad preferred vodka! Oh, I guess in desperation he might have swallowed some Chablis but I'm just the opposite and will sip Smirnoff if I've run out of Two Buck. But this gets to the point that it was tough growing up in a dry town, which Pacific Grove was until 1969. Last town with local prohibition in the state! It all started in yesteryear when the Puritans put their mark on our Piney Paradise. I'm not sure what prompted the City Counsel to change history, but I suspect it was influenced by the Episcopalians and the Catholics. Somehow Communion just wasn't the same with grape juice. My mother explained to me that wine in the Bible was not the same as wine today, and even if it was, Jesus said a little wine was good for the stomach. Now, with a little experience, I realize that Mom was passing on what she had learned from her Congregational heritage and didn't really know what she was talking about. In later years she preferred a good Manhattan and no mention of that in the Bible. And I might add that after 1969 there was very little stomach trouble in Pacific Grove.

But all this dryness was not the hardship you might imagine. Dode's, at the top of Forest, just outside the city line, was handy enough and there was always Cork and Bottle in New Monterey. I guess it was the cultural condition that we struggled with. I mean, it was tough enough learning how to drink – responsibly – when we went away to college or joined the Navy, or both.

If you have ever traveled a dusty road, arrived at your hotel anticipating a cold beer, you can imagine the shocked thirsty libertines checking in to the Forest Hill Hotel finding out they might have to go out to dinner! Or sooner. Iced tea and Coke all well and good, but after all. The old timers knew the ropes, brought their own, or leaned on Luther the Maintenance Man to make a quick run to Dode's. Then the front desk banged the bell, "One Set Up – ice and soda – to 403," and away we went for a two bit tip. We bellhops helped Thelma in Housekeeping lug the empties out in the morning. If there was an ounce or two left in a bottle we saved it for Luther.

Our Monterey friends, living with "old country" traditions, grew up with wine in the basement, called it Italian Red, or something like that. Their parents and grandparents bought barrels of juice at the end of summer and put it to work until spring. When we were of legal age it was easy enough to drive that mile and a half to buy a six-pack for a card game, but there was some fascination about making your own. Some of us tried making home brew – delicious when it worked, but then there were the bottles exploding in the night!

Well, just for the record, Pacific Grove didn't go straight to hell with prohibition lifted. Oh, there are those who would disagree, but they never drank a drop anyway! I'll see you at Trader Joe's!

* * * * *

Give Gophers a Name

OK, I know they were here before we were, but after all! I'm talking now about raccoons, deer, gophers, rats, and any other pests that may intrude on our civilization.

Our friend, Melinda, had a terrible time with gophers, and in addition to being a fantastic musician, she is also a world class gardener, with no tolerance for the little bastards. I suggested she give them a name and learn to love them. She would have none of it!

On a fine sunny afternoon she connected a hose to the exhaust pipe of her BMW, the other end down a fresh gopher hole. Started the car, went in the house, possibly to riffle through "I'll Be Glad When You're Dead, You Rascal You!"

Well, an alert neighbor, having read of carbon monoxide demises, and not noticing the business end of the hose, called 911, and all hell broke loose on the normally peaceful end of Carmel. The cops were first, then the paramedics, followed closely by the fire truck. The deed was done, no citation, but a lecture or two and wagging of fingers. There was some thought to include the SPCA, emergency vet, and the Game Warden, but that would have been over kill, no pun, etc. Not sure if the gopher died or just couldn't stand the racket and left. There was the thought that Robert, Melinda's husband, a poet of some note, might write a verse or two in memory of Georgie Gopher, but that has been discounted.

Now rats are a different breed of cat, so to speak, and unfortunately, they like to eat the same things that we do. They can also mess things up when they decide to camp and set up housekeeping behind the kitchen wall, and their sanitary habits are not compatible with our standards. Again, the naming and learn to love routine solves none of the above. Moving down "Death Row" at Brinton's I discovered the Rat Zapper which I won't describe here, but friends, it is neat, easy, humane and effective. We all know about the snapper which can also be effective, and some people take delight in viewing the remains. Not me! Not me! Then too, the snapper may not kill completely, and that is a real mess.

My friend, Hans, not only a humanitarian but possibly a rodentartian, (kind to rats) traps these little rascals live and relocates them to the hinterland, exact location not disclosed. Usually an easy transport, NPR on the radio, but not too long ago Roger the Rat slipped out of the cage and began to scurry with considerable enthusiasm around Hans' car! Hans pulled to the side of the road, opened the door and verbally encouraged the rat to leave. About this time the sheriff arrived, wondered what was going on! Hans explained, and since this sort of thing happens all time, the sheriff gave assistance and the day ended very well.

In recent months there seems to be a decline in raccoon sightings, which is a very fine thing. I remember when they used to be cute. There is the possibility that we have heeded the advice of animal control, and by not feeding them they have moved on. Then, too, a few weeks ago I spotted a couple of gals swinging down Ocean Avenue wearing, among other things, raccoon caps, complete with tail, a la Davy Crockett. Very possibly imports, or road kill recovery. (Don't make too much of the tail thing.)

You may also recall an item a few months ago on how to cook a raccoon. Don't bother.

Deer? Well most of us like deer, Bambi and all that. Fine photo ops for the visitors, but they have been known to ruin gardens. Best to try the name thing.

In closing, let us remind ourselves that tourists, visitors, or guests, are definitely NOT pests! Sure, they may foul the footpath, park all over the place and leave car doors open, but they are our friends, our excitement, and our livelihood! Give them names, and learn to love them! "Hello, sweetheart! Welcome to the Monterey Peninsula!"

* * * * *

How Now

Flashing back to those fine days of happy silliness, I stumbled on good old How Now Brown Cow. This leads, of course, to the Purple Cow, following. The Brown Cow thing, a delight to recite after a couple of sav blancs, is notable in that it is an example of dipthongs.... That's OK. Neither do I! Nothing to do, I'm sure, with the new thong thing, but might be worth some scrutiny.

Now, on the Monterey Peninsula, we take smug delight in the noted authors, past and present, that at least passed through here. Or stayed. Steinbeck, Stevenson, Calkins, Bowhay, Hemp, Steffens, and Smiley, of course, but not much mention of good old Gelett Burgess! From the pages of Game and Gossip I see that he arrived here in Carmel in 1950, lived on San Antonio, then died in 1951. To his regret, or so he said, was the poem entitled "The Purple Cow: Reflections on a Mythic Beast Who's Quite Remarkable, at Least."

I never saw a purple cow

I never hope to see one:
But I can tell you, anyhow,
I'd rather see than be one!

This gives us some idea of his intellect, and a valuable tool when amusing grandkids.

Burgess worked at UC Berkeley in the 1890s as instructor of topographical drawing, but most of all, he liked to have fun. This included his beheading of Henry Cogswell's statute atop the Cogswell Fountain, a huge cast iron monstrosity given to San Francisco in honor of temperance. The prank caused UC to terminate Burgess, an event which in later years might have resulted in an advanced degree. In fact, he is now held in "high regard" by the university. Amazing what time and death will do.

There is a local angle here, too! Pacific Grove, possibly Thirst Capital of California, was honored by prohibitionist Cogswell, with one of his awful fountains which offended the eye in Jewell Park for many years. In 1942 the pile of cast iron was donated to the scrap drive, and Pacific Grove can take some credit for winning the war. OK. Cogswell, too! Just for the record, an old canon which sat in front of The Museum for a long time, was also sacrificed for victory.

But back to Burgess. You may not remember the Goops, but if you have kids or grandkids, you might want to look them up. Today the Goops would be called "slobs" and the description of their bad manners tells children what Not to do.

The Goops they lick their fingers.
And the Goops they lick their knives!
They spill their broth on the table cloth
Oh, they lead disgusting lives!

Keep in mind this all before Sesame Street. Hard to tell how much he influenced Carmel, or the other way around, but as a writer of brilliant nonsense, we have to wonder. Before his death he had intended to build a nonsense machine in his San Antonio patio, a "contraption which does all sorts of remarkable things, accomplishes absolutely nothing, but is one hundred percent efficient." (Please. Make no connection with local current state of affairs!)

Burgess wrote a lot more than nonsense. His novels, short stories, social commentary, and more, are better than good, but Goops and Purple Cow draw us back.

By the way, he coined the word "Blurb" in 1907. Good story there, but study this next quote before you go to bed tonight. "If in the last few years you haven't discarded a major opinion or acquired a new one, check your pulse. You may be dead."

* * * * *

Tell Me About High School

Back between the good old days and now, I interviewed people who thought they wanted careers in the securities business. Stockbrokers. One fine day a high priced "consultant" suggested that if we wanted to really get into their souls, ask them about high school. The first time I tried this psych technique the lady in front of me burst into tears, blew her nose, shook her head, and walked out, possibly to Merrill Lynch.

Figuring this might have been an aberation, I used this ploy again the next day on a disenchanted insurance salesman. He stood up, made a very impolite remark, and stormed out the door.

This kind of reaction still puzzles me. High school in Pacific Grove was just fine. In fact, it was great! Oh, of course there were the run of the mill problems like frequent apprehension, rejection, embarrassment, loneliness, acne, physical pain, and itches you couldn't scratch, but by and large, life was good! I look through the 1947 yearbook, The Sea Urchin, and I see a pretty happy bunch. Truth to tell, it just might have been that we lived on the Monterey Peninsula, especially Pacific Grove. It seems to me that nobody was rich, and nobody was poor. There wasn't "the other side of the tracks" unless you count the bay. Nobody, and I mean nobody, drove a car to school! And I don't think any families had two cars. When we were old enough to drive we had to pick a night when Mom and Dad wanted to stay home. Maybe listening to the radio, or reading Saturday Evening Post.

I don't know if Barbara Foster's family was "rich" – he was the City Attorney – but they did live in a very upscale house out on The Drive, near the Country Club. If Barbara was "rich," she didn't show it. Not that we would have known the difference, but she was sweet, kind and generous and what a treat to visit her home! Now if I've left out others "well to do." I apologize. They didn't throw it around.

We all had jobs – gardening, canneries, Holman's, Asilomar,

babysitting, Forest Hill Hotel, and plenty more. Our parents didn't seem to worry about drugs, and I don't think we knew what they were. Robert Mitchum did something funny on a yacht, but none of that trickled up or down to Pacific Grove. Or maybe it was Errol Flynn. Or both.

I suppose there's nothing like sixty years to smooth and sort out memories and although I really did grow up in the best of times in the best of places. My kids and grandkids seem to have grown up in pretty good shape, too. Although we struggled with Subject A (English?) we didn't have to worry about SATs and while the colleges were jammed with GI Bills, there was still room for us. OK. Not too tough to get in. A little tougher to stay in, but that's another story!

Can you imagine, a seventeen-year-old kid, buffered from the world in Pacific Grove, on a train, alone, to college in Albuquerque? Now that was a trauma! Well, six years later I had a wife and son, just like a lot of my classmates. And look how well we all turned out! So if you are asked how was high school, tell them!

* * * * *

Teachers

If you have been lucky enough to experience a dinner with somebody from the PGHS Class of 1947 you will no doubt have noticed the impeccable table manners.

I give credit for this social excellence to Mr. Val Clement, our Senior Problems teacher. I suspect kids from Carmel and Monterey grew up knowing which fork to use, but in PG we seemed to be more interested in getting to the bottom of a root beer float with a straw. Well, maybe it was just me. At any rate Mr. Clement explained the nicety of holding the fork in the left hand, the knife in the right, cutting and eating one bite at a time. Never, never cut up the whole piece of meat before eating! And not only that, when finished eating, the knife goes on the plate, sharp edge IN!

"Why?" said Mr Clement. To avoid cutting the servants!

This was before we discovered pizza in our piney paradise, and the only servants we knew were in Gone With The Wind. I confess an occasional lapse these many years later, but try to remain correct when invited to lunch at Pebble Beach, the Country Club, or even Mission Ranch. And Oh! One more thing. Never laugh at Easterners working on an artichoke for the first time! After all, how was your first exposure to soft shell crab?

The other significant gem laid on us by Mr. Clement was How To Write a Check. High school seniors, 1947, had very little experience in this regard, but by golly, when we grew up and needed to pay a bill we sure knew where to put the dollars and cents, not to mention our signatures.

I know it's almost trite to say how much we owe our teachers, and not just what they taught us out of the book, but how they sometimes set us on the right path, and all that. Trite, but true. For stern, but benevolent authority, how about our principal, A. B. Ingham. I seem to remember a tight little smile on his face as he roamed the halls. Once upon a time he noticed two boys trying to sneak a couple of ice cream bars into the library study hall. They stuck them in their pockets, and he said "That's OK boys. Just leave them there!"

Well, as important as cutting your chicken fried steak might be, it didn't come anywhere near preparation for the dreaded English A examination. Saving us from disaster was Miss Vega Swift who most of us remember as the best teacher we ever had. She rode a bike and hiked the John Muir Trail every summer, storing up enough patience to teach us how to diagram a sentence. As good as she was I could never grasp the concept, but managed to pass the test anyway. Possibly on good looks.

Teacher talk always triggers memories and comparisons and I'll leave it to you to remember Miss Gardner, Mrs. Mello, Roger Matthews, Coach Baskin, and on and on. But with a nod to Monterey High, how about Miss Rendtorff? If conversation ever lags when talking to a Toreador, just mention her name… Gertie, they called her. She has been described to me as a sort of Mother Teresa with a whip! Dean of Women she patrolled the halls preaching propriety, allowing no more intimacy than holding hands! A strict chaperone at school dances, she was also a very caring counselor if you needed one. I happen to live in the old Rendtorff home in Carmel and I think she sometimes speaks to me in the dead of night.

And, thank you, Lord, for all those who taught us, and look how well we all turned out!

* * * * *

Bully Beware!

All right, young man! If some bully on the beach kicks sand in your face, with your girlfriend watching, Charles Atlas to the rescue! Dynamic Tension is the answer, and in a few short weeks you'll no longer be a ninety-pound weakling, but a strong stack of muscles just like Atlas himself!

Just for the record, I tried this from age ten to fourteen, and for me it didn't work, but then, nobody kicked sand in my face, either With the current bully epidemic this subject might get some attention. Actually, nothing new about bullies, and most of us ninety-pound weaklings learned the value of diplomacy early on. Then too, I did win my last fight by 100 yards. But bullies have been known to underestimate their target. Sixth grade, Horace Mann Grammar School in Bakersfield, some big guy decided that since I was a teacher's pet, it would be fun to pull my hair and impress the girls. In a split second of blind rage I became a Tasmanian Devil, wolverine and a raging bull! With tears in my eyes and blood on my nose I let into that son of a bitch with a fury he has not forgotten to this day. I pounded, kicked and hollered while the girls cheered on. The bully was a blubbering wreck and was saved from death by the Yard Teacher. As satisfying is the memory, I do deplore violence and strongly urge current victims of harassment to strike back by other means. Ask your parents, kids.

But let's flash back, or forward to more current body builders, or strong men, like Jack LaLanne! Last I heard he's still kicking, lifting, running, and selling juice extractors. Right around ninety-five, and he recovered not too long ago from heart surgery, but still works out every day. He has been called "the godfather of fitness." Check his record, folks, then tell yourself you're too old to work out!

Look back with me to a name you might have forgotten or never knew. Alan "Captain America" Jones. He was stunt man, daredevil, fitness fanatic, but most of all, a patriot. In 1984 he broke the world's record of consecutive parachute jumps in 24 hours – 236! With hands and feet bound he swam the Strait of Juan de Fuca – eleven miles – in 10 hours ad 22 minutes. His specialty was diving, spread eagled, from a diving tower into 6 inches of water, and once jumped into pool of rattlesnakes and piranhas. Sounds nuts to us, but he wanted to prove there are very few limits to what we can do. I met him at the Golden Door, a long time ago, a kind and gentle guy. As a Marine CBullyaptain he was selected as the good will ambassador to the Olympic Games in Munich. He died in a one car accident in 1990 at the age of 43.

We don't have to look very far for strong people today. The Triathalon is just one example. Peek in any gym and see both men and women shoving, lifting, and pulling, building the perfect body, whatever that is. Actually, I prefer the lean, mean, and fast, but a little late for that. On the other hand, just look at our Governor!

* * * * *

How to Build a Fire

Flashing back to the "good old days," loosely defined as those when we were growing up, I realize how much we learned from The Boy Scout Handbook. The gals, I'm sure, had happy exposure to the Girl Scout edition. Those books, right along with Reader's Digest, and earlier, The Weekly Reader, taught us how live happily, with all necessary skills and admonitions, getting ready for Life! Dads, moms and grandparents really did tell us almost everything we had to know before being kicked out of the nest, but those books were there, at the ready, to fill in the blanks. I know, not to leave out the Bible, but it seemed to me there were more "Nots" than "Knots" on the way to salvation.

I bring this up now, since thanks to NPR, I have discovered a book for all stages and ages that covers everything from How to sew on a button, How to Shave, or change the oil in a car. The book is aptly titled "How to Build a Fire, and other handy things your grandfather knew," by Erin Bried. Now friends, I'm not in the book selling business – tough enough trying to sell my own – but first of all, this book is just fun to read. More importantly, it's the perfect gift, birthday or otherwise, for grandchildren of any age, or even their parents! After all, you can only learn just so much on the Internet.

OK, first chapter, "How to Plant a Tree." Then "How to Buy a House," How to Buy a Car," "How to Season a Cast Iron Skillet," "How to Plan a Date," followed by "How to Wear Cologne." (Very carefully)

Unless you live in a construction zone, like Carmel, it has probably been a long time since you had a flat tire. Now with an old Plymouth or Chevy, especially when we were young, nothing to it. Jack it up, spin the wrench, remove the lugs, repeat the process, and away we went. Which reminds me. Over 40 years ago, my wife and I with our two little kids drove over to the Marin General in San Rafael to pick up our beautiful two day old adopted daughter. Very exciting, emotional and tender. With

Baby Carrie snuggled in Mom's arms, kids in the back seat of the Ford Wagon. giggling and grinning. Half way across the Richmond/San Rafael bridge, that awful thump, thump, thump. Closest place to stop about 50 yards across. And friends, me in my coat and tie, I changed that tire, possibly praying and swearing at the same time, quicker than in the pits at Indy. I may have left the hubcap. I point this out since you never know, under what stress, you may have to change a tire. This book spells it out! And Baby Carrie turned out just fine.

And now, if like many of us, you are a grandparent, it's a lot easier to call Triple A.

There's a piece on how to buy a suit, how to wear cuff links, and how to tell a joke! Just so you know, I'm buying at least ten copies, and am alerting River House Books, and The Works in PG, that you might want four or five yourself!

How to write a love letter, how to play bocce ball, how to catch a fish, teach a dog to sit and stay... Oh, Boy!

* * * * *

Halloween!

Maybe you're the kind of Halloweiner that turns off the lights, pulls down the shades and hides in the bedroom. Friend, if that's you, you are missing a lot! You and I may be tired of the old Trick or Treat routine, but for those little three year olds and older sibs this is really big stuff! Maybe you don't remember your first dip into veiled extortion, or maybe you had all the Hershey Kisses you could handle at home. I had never heard of all this free candy until I was eight years old, two thirds of the way through the Great Depression. A pal led me to a nice house on the hill in Bakersfield, "What is this?" He said, "Just say trick or treat!" Well, sure enough! Rang the door bell, the door opened, "Trick or treat!" and a lovely lady ushered us in, and there a table loaded with candy, cakes, and cookies. The hook was set and I didn't miss a Halloween until just about the time my voice was changing and at the first door bell, "Say, aren't you a little old for this sort of thing!"

So back to home base at 18th and Laurel, and I took up the hand out the treat duty.

Years later I shepherded my own kids up and down the neighborhood, pointing out the most promising houses. Then the rainy Halloween when at every home the Dad was forced... yes, forced!... to have a drink! A fun, but long Halloween! My wife insisted that next year she would escort the kids, and I could stay home and pass out the treats.

(Bad choice of words! Better to say *Hand* out the treats.)

There was, and I guess still is, the curmudgeon types who reached in the kid's bag and snapped their fingers, pretending an offering. Worst of all, the jokers who dropped an ice cube in the sack. On the other hand, were folks like you and me who pretended to be afraid and then praised the witches, pirates and ghosts for their clever costumes.

And the line half a block long up to the door of the lady who smiled, and dropped in dollar bills!

Not as many kids roaming around as in the good old days, and that may be just my neighborhood. Shaving cream and soap still a nuisance. with a broken pumpkin here and there.

The little ghosts who can hardly reach the doorbell are just as cute now as they were fifty years ago, and will be just as sick the day after. Moms and Dads will stash away some of the candy, but the kids, all jazzed up on a sugar high, will stay awake far too late. After all, it's tradition!

One of the best, twenty-five years ago, here in Carmel, at the front door, a pretty girl about ten, dressed in a gypsy outfit. Said, "If you give me a treat, I'll dance for you!"

Well, in she came and proceeded to dance for us and our dinner guests, complete with tambourine and castanets, for ten minutes! A very classy kid, and out the door with a Hershey bar, meeting Mom at the curb.

Little gypsy, I'm sure you've grown into a lovely lady, with little dancers of your own.

But if you're in town this Halloween, please come and dance for us, just one more time!

We'll give you a treat! Up to you. White or Red... and candy for the kids!

* * * * *

Hair

One of the advantages of sitting in the back of the church is the ability to witness, and maybe appreciate, the myriad of hairstyles, primarily on the ladies. This is not a fixation of mine, but when it is difficult to hear the preacher it does fill in some of the blanks. This naturally leads to a reverie and recollection of hair in the movies in years gone by. Only a few of us remember Veronica Lake with those lovely blonde locks over her right eye. She was the Peekaboo Girl and her influence is still with us. Her hairstyle was called "the most famous in Hollywood history." You'll notice that Judy Woodruff on NPR almost has it. Just needs another inch.

If you really care about such things, look back at For Whom The Bell Tolls, and you can actually get a trailer on the Internet. There she is! Ingrid Bergman as Maria, with chopped short curls above that beautiful face. Gary Cooper wore a hat. Worth checking out the book again. Something in there about the earth moving.

If you are of a certain vintage you well remember the Shirley Temple curls, forced on girls for a least a generation. And Guy Mitchell sang lustily about an unidentified beauty, whose "hair hung down in ring-a-lets." She was, as I recall, a nice girl, a proper girls, but one of the roving kind.

Some ladies remember the delight of braids and pigtails, around for lots of years. Now the big deal is a ponytail pulled through the back of a baseball cap, and not too many of those in church.

More to the point, remember our local blondes, with peroxide streaks? Then later, beautiful Breck girls? I'm told that if you snuzzled or hugged, the magic scent of Breck was almost overwhelming.

From the back of the church it does seem that the "blue" hair syndrome has faded and that natural gray is now very much in style. Natural white can't be far behind!

We've all known a lot of ladies over the years and darned few have been happy with their hair. Too short, wrong style, wrong color, home perm disaster, split ends, frizz, etc. A friend, a few years back, came home after a session at the beauty parlor, asked a neighbor, "Sally, what do you think of my hair do?"

"Honey," said Sally, "That's a hair *don't*!"

Now, a blessed word to those lucky gals with lovely, natural hair, who do not gild the lily nor mess with perfection. They rinse and comb, forgive a little color, toss their heads with seeming abandon, those silky strands... oh, well, you know what I mean.

Seems to me that back in the not too dark ages, there was hair piled high upon the head, called a beehive. Please don't correct me if I'm wrong. Makes me itch just to think about it. Raised hell with the hat business.

And now, of course, we see that casual "don't give a damn" look – seldom seen in church – sort of a Medusa thing. Well, notice I haven't said a thing about some of the gentlemen. Ah, the gene pool, and luck of the draw! And forgive me if I close with "Hair today, gone tomorrow!"

*   *   *   *   *

Happy Birthday, *etc.*

Having just enjoyed another birthday, I flash back to some of many years ago. Some folks claim modesty in wanting recognition of their birth ignored. Not me! I don't need a brass band every March 12, but modest or not, I enjoy those cards, E-mails, phone calls and multi candled cake. I admit to forgetting birthdays of others, but I'm thinking of an annual day to include all those I know in one mass mailing. I think it makes more sense, however, to remember our moms on our own birthdays. If they're still with us, they will call, but get there first. "Thanks, Mom. I *really* appreciate what you went through on the day I was born!" You can add a Happy Birthday, and tell her thanks for all those years since. If she has passed away, a quiet prayer will be just right. Do it again on Mother's Day.

Grandma Bowhay was born in a covered wagon in the middle of the King's River on Christmas Day. I don't imagine that was a lot of fun, but still a great story. My mom was also a Christmas kid, so we celebrated with her in the middle of July.

I'll skip over mine last year since your feelings might be hurt if you weren't included, but the one in 1936 was a real winner. Paper poppers, Tail on the Donkey, and Musical Chairs. Big chocolate cake, but one of the mothers sent a banana since her kid was diabetic. Turned out *everybody* wanted a banana, which were in short supply. Yes, we have no bananas, and you know the rest. Nice party, but a few hurt feelings.

There are lots of special birthdays, and you know what I mean. We're moving up on another special one, and that brings me to adoption. My mother was adopted by the Philbricks of Pacific Grove sometime around 1910. Mom was the youngest of five girls. Her mother was blind from a childhood accident in Alsace Lorraine. She and her husband had moved to San Francisco a few years before the 06 quake. When he died of a heart attack the girls were placed in the Catholic orphanage on Van Ness. Mom grew up in PG. She called her parents Aunt Flora and Uncle

Sumner, and wonderful parents they were, and that's another story.

Mom loved all her grandchildren, but had a special bond with our youngest daughter, Carolyn, who was also adopted. Carrie had the usual and understandable questions about her "birth mother," but Grandma hugged her and told her about the love of her "real" parents, which she already knew, and still does. Carrie was an awesomely beautiful baby, from day three when we brought her home. Today, over 45 years later, she is lovely woman, and still beautiful.

We talked to her early about the wonderful lady who chose to give her life, and not easy in those days for an unwed pregnancy. While we have certainly wondered and blessed her, we have respected her privacy. A nineteen-year-old college student from the mid west, we knew that she was bright and talented and had all the traits necessary for a good life. Of course, she knows who and where we are, and pleased, we hope, with the Bowhay Google posts. Carrie's birthday is very close now, and sometimes falls on Mother's Day. Each year we thank Kay for her inestimable gift.

* * * * *

R.I.P.

This being our perfect time of year, it's difficult to find a nice, quiet place that isn't overrun with out of town guests. Tourists. Fortunately we have a couple of beautiful, peaceful cemeteries where you can gather your thoughts, meditate, reflect, and wonder.

These special parks are not just for the dearly departed. Lots of stories over the years and flashing back, that's where some of us learned to drive. Having learned to drive, we also found the cemetery a quiet and slightly private place to park with our current honey and discuss the nature of things. "Gather ye rosebuds while ye may, old time is still a flying... " English majors could, with some smug pretension, recite the whole poem, if necessary, but I understand that that was usually enough. If not, "The grave's a fine and private place, but none, I think, do there embrace." Then, of course, there was always The Point, taking our chances with the foghorn. (Pretentious? Moi?)

Pacific Grove's El Carmelo Cemetery is a real gem, kept neat and green, bordered on two sides by the golf course, and across the street from the lighthouse. Leave flowers, if you like, but by the time you're back to the car, the deer have chewed them up. The fog and the sound of the surf are just right. Once in awhile a golf ball bounces off a headstone and a frantic "Fore!" rings through the cypress, but nobody seems to mind.

In Monterey we have two fine cemeteries, San Carlos, and Cementerio El Encinal, right next to each in one very broad expanse. San Carlos dates back to 1834, associated with "the second mission of Father Junipero Serra." This seems to be more traditional with acres of tombstones and monuments, while El Encinal, owned by the city of Monterey, has broad lawns and massive oaks. Both are perfect for peaceful meditation and memory. A friend, when overwhelmed with stress, comes here to rest, remember, and to restore her soul.

On the north side near Dennis the Menace, the Monterey Cross, old and rugged, has been resurrected and stands in quiet dignity.

Cemeteries have a special fascination if you are genealogically interested, or a history buff. Then, too, some of the epitaphs are worth collecting. The headstone of a hypochondriac says simply, "I Told You So!"

I suppose it's not just fraternities that borrow flowers for whatever reason, but there is the rationalization these blossoms should get some further use before they wilt. (Dear old Mom, Dad, or Uncle John would certainly approve!)

I read recently that some cemetery up North – possibly Catholic – with excess space between the graves – planted grapes in long rows, and I think that would be a very fine vineyard for interment!

There is that old "whistling in the grave yard" humor. Stories about the minister who, with eyes closed in prayer, stepped back and fell into the open grave, and from then on concentrated on weddings. A friend tells me that if you're very quiet you can hear the faint sound of pacemakers still beeping away.

Well, the old guy who said, "If I can't take it with me, I'm not going!" was wrong. Sooner or later... well, you know the rest.

*   *   *   *   *

Speak to Me!

Flashing back again to the good old days, I think it was Mom who said, "It's not so much what you say... It's how you say it!" Or maybe it was how you sound. Great advice, of course, but that takes me to voices!

Despite the recent chatter about NPR, I have to recognize for those of us who have ears to hear, the sounds, both sibilant and otherwise, courtesy of KAZU. Sure, there are those chronically depressed who won't listen to 90.3, but ah, what a loss! To them, at any rate! An hour with Terry Gross and "*Fresh Air*" will heal the sin sick soul. I never had a teacher that sounded that good, and who knows what might have become of me! And now, when she says *Fresh Air,* I don't care *what* she says. She's talking to me!

NPR doesn't have the corner on special voices, but I think they have most of them. How about Lynne Rossetto Kasper who chats about food on "The Splendid Table." She is warm and confidential, talking to those of us who like to eat, and on Saturday afternoon it's a lovely way to drift into a slumber, dreaming of minestrone.

For anyone who has recently suffered a rejection, Krista Tippett will make it all OK. Smooth, spiritual, sincere, and you can almost hear that soft smile.

Contradicting Mom for a moment, Diane Rehm proves what you say is more important than how it sounds. Diane suffers from a vocal cord disorder, Spasmodic Dysphonia, and gets regular injections in her throat to control the spasms. Sometimes a little rough on the edges, and maybe a little halting, she is brilliant and speaks with quiet authority and you can almost hear her courage.

Robin Young, "Here and Now," speaks with just the right amount of self assurance, and there is a pleasant lilt as she moves through our daily trauma, and always reassuring. Robin's *Here and Now*, almost like *Fresh Air,* happily sets up the rest of the morning.

Speaking of courage, how about Julie Andrews with that pure silver voice, wrecked with unfortunate vocal cord surgery. She and her daughter, Emma, have collected and written poems, songs, and lullabies in a beautiful book, but better than that, a CD is included. Even if she can't yet hit the high notes, Julie's voice, strong and soft, sweet and lyrical, reads the verses you will remember your mom reading to you a long time ago.

Now how about everybody's uncle or grandfather, Walter Cronkite. You can hear him again on the Internet and remember why he was "the most trusted man in America." When he signed off with, "and that's the way it is," you knew for sure, that's the way it was.

Friends, if I'd had a voice like Hal Riney's I would never have been a stockbroker!

Remember, "It's Morning Again, in America!" Say it one more time, Hal. We need it!

And "It's morning, in Washington Square. Coffee, Mario's, and the Chronicle."

OK... just ask me. I'll try.

How about "It's morning... on Wharf Number 2... my coffee at LuLu's... reading the Herald."

To wind this up on a happy note, how about Red Barber! A real gentleman and knew baseball, along with camellias and was pleased to both announce and philosophize on either. And then possibly the best sports announcer in history, how about Bill King!

Sharp, smart, and perfectly dramatic. And if you haven't done it lately, tune in through the Internet to Russ – Bye Bye Baby – Hodges! When you flipped on the radio and heard his voice, and that old champion, Lon Simmons, you knew it was Giants Baseball! I know. Lon did the 49ers, too. Lots more, but you can tell, when I start a story I have no idea where it will end. But just one more thing, as Columbo used to say. Crank up the Internet again. Get all those voices above, and then get the Giants

Fight Song! You remember! "When the Giants come to town, it's Bye Bye Baby!"

Just in time for spring training!

* * * * *

Going Up!

As the story goes, Elisha Otis, in the late 1800s, developed a box sort of device that moved people sideways, to the right and left. It just didn't sell.

One day a friend said, "Elisha, how about having it move people up and down!" Well, as they say, the rest is history. Actually, elevators of a sort have been around long before Otis, but he did develop a safety system that kept them from falling all the way down the shaft. Otis now, is almost a generic term for "the lift," dominant worldwide.

This all came to mind the other evening when, at a very classy event, several of us got stuck in an elevator. Not stuck, really, but the door closed, the car wouldn't budge, and the door wouldn't open. I guess that is stuck.

Since this was a very classy crowd, there was very little panic, although as the seconds ticked away, the air getting thick with perspiration – sweat, actually – the dozen of us began to get concerned. Who, for instance, would just lose it, and start to scream. Fortunately most of us had had a glass or two of wine, and some even saw the humor in the situation. One little lady politely tapped on the elevator door, saying softly "Hello? Hello?"

But then the lady in charge bravely opened the emergency phone, just as if there was an emergency, dialed the emergency number, and on the speaker, the response was "If you would like to make a call...." In the meantime those passengers with an engineering background, pushed all the buttons, all to no avail. After what seemed like an hour and half, (actually maybe five minutes) somebody outside decided they wanted to go up, pushed the up button, the door opened, we bravely walked out, and took the stairs.

I have a certain interest in elevators since back in the good old days, as a bellhop in the venerable Forest Hill Hotel, the pride of Pacific Grove, we ran the Otis up and down, five floors up, and down the shaft to the basement.

Pacific Grove was a little short on elevators, and I guess still is. A couple at Holman's, of course, but the real class conveyance was the Forest Hill Otis.

Linoleum floor, with a brass Otis in the center, wood paneling, and a nice little table in the corner, handy to hold room service when necessary. The doors, with obscure glass, opened and closed with hand pulled levers. There was nothing automatic, the ups and downs controlled by hand on a handle, driven by highly skilled bellhops. We took great pride in zooming up and down at full speed, skidding to a stop at exactly the right level.

I reluctantly admit riding on top of the elevator, on quiet nights, with visiting girl friends, and even more reluctantly admit crouching in the bottom of the shaft as the car stopped three feet above us. Two large springs, almost three feet high, were our margin of safety. The girl from Indiana, a guest at the hotel with her parents – more about her later – grabbed my arm, me in my maroon uniform with the grey stripes, said "Oh, I'm scared!" She later admitted that she wasn't scared at all, but just wanted to hug me.

You can understand my appreciation of elevators. Truth to tell, my sweetheart, did indeed, squeeze my hand in the stuck elevator above. After climbing the stairs, another glass of wine seemed appropriate.

* * * * *

The High Cost of Cleanliness!

A friend of mine, who is very conscious and concerned about our energy waste, has designed a clever apparatus for home use in drying laundry. It seems that ten percent of our energy – gas or electricity – is blasted through our dryers. Or so she has heard. I believe her, since I couldn't otherwise pay PG&E as much as I do on just lights and the oven.

Now back in the good old days we had clotheslines, both inside and out, but mostly out. These were sometimes strung between houses with a pulley arrangement, in the side yard between posts, or in a revolving set up around a pole. Visiting China Town in San Francisco you see laundry like holiday banners blowing from lines strung up from balconies and window frames.

I read that some high end neighborhood in Southern California filed a serious complaint against a thrifty family who hung their sheets out in the breeze. Some concern, I think, about property values, and indeed, look what has happened in the last couple of years!

It was an accepted, and not unpleasant, part of our lives in Pacific Grove back in the forties, and of course, earlier. Fill the laundry basket with the damp, soap smelling combination of shirts, sheets, towels, diapers, and underwear and out to the line with a stand at hand to hold the basket. The clothespins were usually still on the line from yesterdays wash. There was a certain finesse in folding over a sheet, pinning at one corner, and then the other, and it was a real art to hang lots of diapers with as few as possible clothes pins. Underwear, with modest concern, fit nicely between the dishtowels, and if it was a nice warm breezy day, the whole load would be dry by dinner time. Now I know how nice it is to pull a warm sheet out of dryer, but there was something wholesome and natural about the smell of a sun dried sheet, and yes, even a diaper.

From down the street the summer sweetheart would stop by to help me take in the laundry, a summer game to take down the same sheet from the opposite side. Both tugging, laughing, then hugging, the sheet between us. Ah, the smell of the sun dried sheet! It doesn't work the same with a Kenmore.

Now this is all well and good if you live and wash in Carmel Valley, or even Southern California, but around here we do get these strung out periods of fog and a shortage of sunshine. This bring us to the subject of inside clothes lines and drying racks which are not fun nor convenient. Oh, a towel or two is OK, but with sheets, socks, and T-shirts strung between bedrooms and the upstairs hall there is a desire to do the laundry a little less often. Remember, too, that in those days people smoked.

With concern for the planet, PG&E, and my budget I invested in a length of clothesline, determined to re live the good old days. But then, with concern for the neighbors' property values, I left the line in the garage. I'll have to do a little cost analysis on the use of my electric dryer and a few quarters at the Laundromat. After all, my time is worth something. And then, I'm probably better off waiting for my friend to develop her home drying apparatus. Or maybe change sheets every other week!

*   *   *   *   *

Books!

Every once in awhile I flash back to Jimmy Durante doing "I'll Never Forget The Day I Read A Book." Of course you and I will never forget Dick and Jane and their pal, Spot.

I have a hunch you might find a tattered copy in the kid's section of Pacific Grove Library, just to the right as you walk in the door. On those days when you feel a little tattered and torn yourself, tired of television and think maybe Chicken Little is right, take a library break, stroll in and look around. There is peace and excitement, all at once. A walk through the stacks, touching some of those familiar old names we grew up with, will settle the soul and rekindle some of that old interest in reading.

Once upon a time a teacher explained that by ourselves, we can live only one life, but in a library we are able to live thousands of lives and experiences. And sure enough! With thanks to Andrew Carnegie (you could look it up...) I saw the wonders of the world with Richard Halliburton, sailed around the world with Jules Verne, visited OZ with Frank Baum, and stayed up nights with the Hardy Boys, Tom Swift, and on and on.

There still remains that quiet and friendly authority of the librarians who pointed out sections, collections, and special authors that were always just right. All librarians are, by definition, beautiful, but they are also teachers, house mothers, guides, directors, and friends. It must have something to do with exposure to all those books.

If you haven't been to the library lately you might not remember that subtle smell, the almost pungent, but not quite, odor of books. You can close your eyes and know where you are. No, not the scent of other readers, it's the history of the million pages, right there! And library paste! Of course!

You may remember banned books, and you may remember "Memoirs of Hecate County," by Edmund Wilson. Tough, in the good old days, to get the real read on "the facts of life." The word was that this book spelled it out, and hence, banned! Well, sooner or later it showed up on then "restricted" shelf of Pacific Grove Library, and I forget whatever subterfuge I used, but I took it home. Friends, don't bother. Sure, well written, but after all!

There is so much now to read, the lure of the "Best Sellers," flashy jackets, not only lurid, sensitive, and deep, but think of the authors we missed along the way. They are there, waiting, calling to us! Check me out, or sit right down in that leather chair, and feel the touch of the pages! It's free!

And if your soul is flat, take a look at the kids... reading!

* * * * *

Double Your Pleasure

Amazing how a little research can shoot down a good story. Great plans for the old chewing gum flavors, now gone with the good old days. Juicy Fruit, Beemans, Clove, and Black Jack. Gone? Nope. Just wander into Bruno's in Carmel, and there they all are! Juicy Fruit, next to Doublemint, a little different packaging, not to mention the price, but same old sickeningly sweet flavor. The only thing missing, but maybe I didn't look hard enough, was good old Fleers, the gold standard bubble gum with the funny paper wrapping!

Not too sure where to follow up on gum, but I seem to remember parents saying "Chew this, and shut up!" That just before carsick. Well, Beemans was the worst, tasted like medicine, and maybe it was. Of course, as kids, we chewed tar from the roofers and pitch from the pine trees. And then the paraffin lids from Mom's canning, or best yet, the wax lips with the penny candy along with AbbaZabba or jellybeans before the matinee. Depending on the depth of your puppy love, you could share your Doublemint with your sweetie. I mean, she chews for five minutes, transfers the glob to you, and this well before H1N1.

Now don't tell me you didn't know what to do with the tired chicle. The story that it didn't digest for seven years if you swallowed it, false! Remember the kid in front of you in class, stuck it behind his ear! And I really don't want to think about it, but still, friends, just run your finger under the library table, or the desk, or Aunt Martha's dining room furniture. This takes me to the local sidewalks. Actually, not too bad. Bad enough in Singapore where gum is outlawed, unless bought by prescription! This because used gum was being disposed of endangering public safety. Well!

You'll have to look it up!

Don't know what's up in Connecticut, but in Hartford a dramatic increase in shoplifted gum, and not just stick or two. Now just in case I haven't ruined your morning, chewing gum art and yes, even sculptures, at least in England and Venice, and you know that San Francisco can't be far behind.

Well, the good news is that chewing gum can indeed, be good for your teeth, breath, digestion, attitude, and health in general. Some report that chewing during a math test helps your score. And look what it's done for baseball!

Remember when most of our news came from The Weekly Reader? Now, just log on! I'll save the discovery to you, but if it's a slow day, look up the ten top gum flavors in Japan. Better yet, play those Japanese gum commercials. Never mind, Wrigley. We'll stick with Juicy Fruit!

* * * * *

Lovely Old Ladies

Among the many tastes on earth that are seldom acquired are horehound drops. A brown, sugar dusted candy, usually kept in cut glass dishes by old ladies who often came from New England and insisted it was good for you. Take my word, horehound tastes awful, sort of a cross between burnt coffee, cod liver oil, and the way cat piss smells. Don't try it.

I bring this up because when I was a little boy my mother would take me to visit old ladies in musty houses knowing that they would smile and tell her what a special little boy I was. Of course, and look how I turned out! But that's another story.

Despite the horehound, most of these old lady houses were not only interesting, but in some cases, downright fascinating. Mrs. Swann lived around the corner from our house in San Luis Obispo. Brown shingles, two ratty palm trees in the front yard, and a jungle of split leaf philodendron in the entry hall. The place was always stuffy hot, gas heater hissing in the corner, horehound in the cut glass dish on the doily covered table. I would have forgotten all this except for the icon on the fireplace mantle. A clear glass bottle, about six inches tall, formaldehyde, and her dead mother's ring finger, complete with wedding ring. It was tied with a small bow at the base, and pale fingernail at the top. No flowers to soften the image, no picture of the departed, just an otherwise bare mantle with Mama's digit. While Mrs. Swann explained casually what this was and then moved on to other things, I was transfixed and stared at this thing without comment. My mother, who was just as fascinated, and possibly repelled, had the sense not to tell me not to stare. And horehound or not, I always looked forward visiting Mrs. Swann. I don't remember if there were any offspring of Mrs. Swann who might have inherited the finger, but would rather hope that it was buried along with Mrs. Swann, unless, of course, she was herself preserved in some other unorthodox manner.

Back in Pacific Grove, the Old Lady Capitol of the World, the old lady houses were just as fascinating, but not quite as bizarre. The cut glass dishes had those little flat chocolate drops mixed in with the horehound, but the houses were just as hot, sometimes with a cat curled in the corner and huge houseplants in late stages of life. Miss Eglantine Preble was especially nice and interesting. Commodore Preble who battled the Barbary pirates from the USS Constitution, "Old Ironsides," was her grandfather and she told us tales of our early navy, New England whalers, and the Maine coast. She had a little doll named Hitty, supposedly immortalized in Rachael Field's book, *Hitty, Her First Hundred Years.*

Hitty's first owners were the Prebles. Miss Preble gave us a copy of the book, still here, next to the family Bible.

And then there were the Tuck sisters, Sue Estelle and Ella. Twins, but Sue Estelle big, and Ella small. They claimed to be distant cousins of the Philbricks, but who isn't. Ella was a good artist and I still have a small seascape she gave us for a wedding gift. Sue Estelle claimed to have super natural powers and read fortunes from a glorious crystal ball, kept in a black velvet bag when not in use. Most fortunes were happy, usually with a caution or two, pointed at clean living and trust in the Lord. My mother dragged one of my semi-serious girl friends to have her fortune told and while the reading was vaguely noncommittal, Sue Estelle later told my mother that she should discourage any long term relationship since the girl's first two children would be stillborn! The relationship was terminated, but for other reasons. Needless to say I have sometimes wondered how things did turn out.

I probably didn't appreciate it at the time, but the Tuck's house was a real museum, loaded with New England artifacts and relics from all over the world. Dinner one night, best tasting taglarini, an off brand pasta casserole popular in Pacific Grove at the time, Happened to walk through the kitchen to use the bathroom – overhead oak tank with pull chain – and saw the sink! It was wooden, black with mold and strange green things growing from the cracks. The dishcloth had an evil looking orange looking – dare I say slime – oozing from beneath. I looked no further, hurried back to the table, and had a second helping of taglarini. None the worse for wear.

*   *   *   *   *

As the Days Dwindle Down

Just a flash back reminder, friends, that Reunion Time is sneaking up on us once again. Sure, you know that reunions are the biggest cause of weight loss in the country, and not many weeks now to work off a pound or two, but a little tune up is probably all we need. Those of us in the seriously mature crowd have the faces we deserve anyway and a face without some lines or wrinkles indicate a life not fully lived! Of course, a very robust trunk is another story. A wide Talbott tie might help. For you more recent graduates, still time for a Botox tune up, but just remember that those Angelena Jolie pillow-lips don't look good on everybody. (Oh, heck. Why not,)

I know. You swore you'd never go through one of those reunions, again, but after all! Maybe you want to show off a new honey, or let them all know that you're still with the old one, who, you might add, still looks good!

Break out the old class yearbook and just think who might show up. Sad to remember those who checked out (died) since the last reunion, and although I hate mention it, this might be the last time you get to see some of your old pals.

One of my favorite reunion stories – names available on request – a gal who was lovely in high school and fifty years later absolutely beautiful. At a reunion a few years ago one of her classmates asked if she'd like to dance.

She, with a smile, I might add, said "You wouldn't ask me to dance then, and I won't dance with you now!"

Now the name thing is always tough, and with any luck there will be name tags. The guys, however, can get away with "Sweetheart!," or "Gorgeous!," or "Well, my! Just look at you now!"

Honesty is safer, especially if the lady so addressed is from Portland and married to a classmate just last year. You'll be forgiven with a nice

"Help me out, I'm Phil Bowhay." No, no! Use your own name! This is just an example!

One of the nice things about growing up in this neck of the woods is that there was very little social or economic class distinction in the good old days. Nobody rich, nobody poor, and nobody lived on "the other side of the tracks." Sure, Barbara Foster – her dad was PG City Attorney – lived out near the Country Club, and what a thrill to be invited to her home, but there wasn't an ounce of pretension in the Foster family.

Well, these many years since we grew up and out, and maybe lucky enough to live back here, some got more merit badges, initials after names, maybe even a lottery winner or two, but the class reunion, one more time, is the great equalizer. Hey! I knew you when… you wet your pants; got caught; dropped that pass!; forgot your lines!; flunked English A! But then, too, I remember you so beautiful at the Senior Dance; when you sunk the winning basket; sang that thrilling solo; were nice to everybody; gave that perfect speech at graduation, and voted Best of Something Important! Best of all, we grew up together, and were friends!

* * * * *

Resolutions

Flashing back over lots of New Years I have asserted my independence by resisting resolutions. To prove the point I usually wait until February to alter my life style. I am reminded of the first Sunday in January many years ago, Piedmont Community Church.

The preacher, Sam Lindamood, questioned resolutions kept or not, and this prompted a very nice lady, although low on her meds, to walk up to the pulpit, give her name, and in strong voice, simply said "B...S...!" My eight-year-old daughter thought this possibly "Contemporary Worship," although there was no guitar accompaniment. Sam's sermon may well have been his best, but none of the congregation heard a single word.

I am not that critical of resolutions, but looking around my house I am appalled by the clutter, some Holiday left over trash, but mostly years of not wanting to throw anything away. I find it *almost* impossible to toss old New Yorkers. I once papered a bathroom wall with New Yorker covers, and for years clipped out cartoons. This morning, looking for unpaid bills I dug through a two foot stack of the magazines – no unpaid bills – and realized I had a similar stack on my bed stand, living room coffee table, and even by that collection of old 78s! After a moment of serious meditation, I remembered that every single New Yorker ever printed is available on DVD! Huzzah, and after several trips to the recycle bin – no hernia, but some lower back pain – I feel liberated!

Now friends, think how good you will feel when you lug out those hundreds of *National Geographic*, some dating back over a hundred years. Every single one is available on a DVD! And Good Grief, W*orld Book Encyclopedia*! Digitally enhanced on the Internet! The kids can even print pictures for their reports!

Having studied the subject I don't think you want to toss that mint collection of Playboys, although I understand that The Best of Playboy is available in some format.

Actually we don't really need Playboy any more. Those interesting articles are at hand somewhere, but that's another story.

Now before we get too whipped up, hurling everything hither and yon, may I suggest we keep in a dry, cool place all our old Readers Digests. After all, we grew up with those attitudes, facts, fiction, and condensed books. Once upon a time RD was the number one selling publication in the world, and was out sold only by The Bible. It was noted, however, that The Bible had a head start. If you really care about Readers Digest, check out the December 19, 2009 story in *The New York Times*, by David Segal. Yep, it's on the Internet. Fascinating story, perfect journalism, and just a darned good read!

And those old 78s? Well, some more of that another time.

* * * * *

Bent Twig

Flashing back on where we were then and where we are now, some seemingly minor events turned into habits. Some of these quirks can be labeled superstitions, but no matter. We move through life tossing spilled salt over our left shoulder with the right hand, and so what! Can't hurt, and who knows?

This not in the same category as brushing teeth, blowing nose, saying prayers and other actions part of the human condition. It's the "add-ons" that I'm talking about. Last week, down Ocean Ave with my daughter, we walked on opposite sides of a tree. "Bread and butter," she murmured, and I didn't bother to ask why. After all, either a superstition or a habit, maybe both. Fortunately, my mother never broke her back after those rare occasions when I stepped on a sidewalk crack.

And speaking of Mom, early advice can stick, become a habit, and shape our personalities. When I was three or four my mother, after a small bout of shyness, told me that Everybody, yes *everybody*, would want to hear whatever I had to say. Now that took a year or two to settle in, but take, it did and with mostly positive results, I never really shut up after that. It became a *habit* to talk, explain, and entertain. Tough habit to break... worse than smoking.

My Dad explained to me at one early part in my life that it was *good* luck to put on and tie your left shoe first... and of course *bad* luck to put on and tie your right shoe first. Well, born skeptic, I tied the right shoe first, and sure enough, bad day, bad luck. I don't remember how bad, but bad enough to convince me that Dad knew what he was talking about... and I developed a habit of putting on the left shoe first. And Good Luck, mostly, from then on.

I recently took a DMV "behind the wheel driving test," seriously mature, etc. I explained to the examiner – nice guy – that despite proper use of the turn indicators, I still had the *habit* of sticking my arm out, just like the old days in the green Chevy. He said that was OK, but slightly complicating since to stick an arm out the window, only one hand left on the wheel, and you know, of course, the two hand requirement. I did get my license renewed. Note that other drivers smile at my friendly wave. And flashing back, remember those awkward "Neckers Nobs?" If you don't, it's not important.

When I was just a baby my Mom would give me a bath, then stand me on the toilet, lid closed, to towel me dry. This ritual continued until I was old enough to take my own bath, but it still seemed natural – a habit – to stand on the toilet to dry. No great note in the high school gym since we all stood on benches after shower to avoid Athlete's Foot.

(What ever became of Athlete's Foot?) This concern kept me off the floor through college and even the Navy. Then about six months into marriage, my wife, Susie, asked "Why do you always stand on the toilet after you get out of the shower?"

I started to explain, but thought better of it, and simply said "It's just a habit."

Easier to break than I thought.

* * * * *

Felice Cumpleaños

Special birthdays, like Christmas and your own, flash us back to where we were on a special or particular one, some recent, some long ago. What happened, who was there, happy, sad, or just another day. I have experience with eighty of my own birthdays, some with parties, special dinners, usually with friends, but this last one, shared with my baby brother, who is only sixty, really took the cake! Contrived and planned by our kids and sweeties, it was a production right out of the movies, and then some. Having shared in several toasts with glass held high, I turned around, and there were The Bay Belles, otherwise known as The Dish and the Dishettes! I held myself together through Happy Birthday, but then dissolved into a blubbering wreck, tears running right down to my necktie, as they did Lida Rose and some other gems. Then they tripped out into the night, looking like a million bucks in their red and white striped vests. Wow! Now That was a birthday to remember!

Most of us tried to do something special on our birthdays, like George Bush jumping out of an airplane. On my fortieth I ran around Lake Merritt, twice. On my most recent I walked around the block... once... then took my nap.

But how about those a long time ago, when we pinned the tail on the donkey, pulled the tab on the popper and put on paper hats! Moms made and frosted the cakes themselves, poked in the candles, told us to make a wish, but not to tell, and then we huffed and puffed with a minimum of slobber. One second grade party, a diabetic kid's mom brought a banana since he couldn't eat sweets. All well and good, except that all the kids wanted a banana instead of cake! This was the party when sweet Eleanor Chalmers, mentioned in earlier stories, gave me a flashlight. Presents always a problem since these were Depression years and some kids just didn't show up, not able to afford a gift. In later years we swung at piñatas, almost as frustrating as proper placement of the tail on the donkey. I think I remember those parties, early in puberty, when some of the girls giggled us into Spin The Bottle, with disappointing results.

Well, in the good old days birthday parties were simple and fun, and then as the world changed, along came clowns and magicians. Hey! Happy Birthday, and off to the bowling alley, or those party palaces with slides and trampolines! Fairylands and Petting Zoos, or the Golden Arches with plastic balls, padded walls, "bouncing parties" and a billion germs! I'm no critic of "wretched excess," but for a little perspective on the current birthday business, which is BIG, take an Internet look at Birthday Parties. No, nobody jumps out of a cake, but some kids look like they just jumped in! Bring back the tail on the donkey!

And now, those clever cards, some on the Internet and some in the mail, all cheerful, some slightly insulting, but fun, and you can always get even when their birthday hits. One more thing. If your Momma is still around, be sure to call and congratulate and thank her – look how well you turned out! If Mom is gone, just close your eyes for a moment, and say Thanks. She will hear you.

And oh, yeah! Happy Birthday!

＊　＊　＊　＊　＊

Are We There Yet?

If memory serves me, it seems that in the good old days we traveled around, mostly by car, or maybe the Greyhound Bus. The ads said "Next Time Try the Train!" and we did when we could. The Del Monte Express, of course, and farther up and down the coast the Southern Pacific Daylight. We connected in LA with Santa Fe, across the country. One thing about the bus, you got to know fellow travelers very well. Sometimes too well. Like flying today. But car trips were the big deal. Into the Chevy, Dad and Mom in the front seat, and we kids in back. On cool days, all the windows were rolled up, and Dad went through a pack of Camels by the time we got to Paso Robles. We shouted out the Burma Shave signs and counted the barns painted with Mail Pouch Tobacco. We got free maps at Standard Oil stations, and that collection of watercolors, I think, featuring the National Parks, or other great sights of The Golden West. No In-N-Out, or MacDonalds, but better yet, lots of root beer and Giant Orange!

This was all before we were called "house guests," but all our trips were lined up toward friends and relatives. Believe me, they did the same when they passed within a hundred miles of Pacific Grove. We were expected to stop by, spend the night, and get caught up. As younger kids we slept three in a bed, the one in the middle with head at the bottom, with two feet on either side. Not good, but better than sleeping on the floor. Well, maybe not. The baby, and it seems we always had one, slept in a dresser drawer. Don't know about you, but our relatives always had a bathroom. Just one. And some of them had quite a few kids. Modesty out the door!

Our trips were always "educational," all the way from Luther Burbank Gardens in Santa Rosa, up to the redwoods above Eureka, with an Arrow shirt factory in between. Other times across the state, stopping at Ernie Still's ranch this side of Blackwell's Corner and old friends then in Bakersfield. Ah, Arizona, with pueblos and petrified forests, and on the way back, Boulder Dam.

Most cars had a canvas bag of water hanging on the front bumper, and it was a lot easier to change a tire then than now. No air conditioning, but a Sears heater under the dash, connected through to the radiator warmed, at least, those in the front seat. My Dad had plugged in a second hand Philco radio, rescued from some junk yard, which happily responded when hit with a closed fist. Best radio story, driving with the radio on – a Motorola – from La Jolla to Palm Springs, my five-year-old daughter asked, "How does the radio know we're in Palm Springs instead of La Jolla?"

Tough to explain to a little kid.... "Well, honey. It just does!" (Lazy parent.)

*　*　*　*　*

The Old Kit Bag, Revisited

Don't you wish you had a dime for every backpack walking around the country? Used to call them knapsacks and I don't think in the good old days any kid would have dared pack one to school. They are, of course, a fine innovation, despite claims of permanent back damage. Looks like some are strapped on kids before they can walk, but in the long run, I guess it might help their posture. I haven't figured what's in them, other than books, cell phones and video games, but maybe lunch.

As I have admitted earlier, memory is a flawed reference, but I don't think we had cafeterias at Pacific Grove Grammar or High School, and that brings me to paper bags and lunch boxes. Most of the time we ran home for a quick bite and then back to school, but on those other days we toted the lunch bucket, packed with loving surprises. Ah, remember the little thermos jugs, just right for soup – Campbell's Tomato – or hot chocolate. (Kept hot things hot, and cold things cold! How did it know!) Maybe a cookie, but the classic, of course, was the sandwich! Two pieces of white Wonder Bread, yellow mustard, and a slice of baloney in between, neatly wrapped in waxed paper. Remember waxed paper? The carrot sticks went into the landfill.

Earlier on, aside from the paper bags with your name penciled in, it was the standard black box, but somewhere along the line came the boxes with Porky Pig, Flash Gordon, Mickey Mouse, and Cinderella. Should have kept them, friend. Worth big bucks today! Just log on and look up Lunch Boxes! You can even smell the baloney. OK, so your Mom preferred peanut butter, maybe cheaper, maybe better for you.

While researching the subject I discovered on the good old Internet a recipe for Roast Baloney! A whole baloney, scored and slathered with yellow mustard and brown sugar, baked for three hours! No baloney! Well, possibly close to baked Spam which still tastes pretty good.

If you grew up in a cafeteria school, you'll remember that tasty glop that later became known as Sloppy Joe. And chipped beef on toast. SOS! Try it today! Great with ketchup. Bakersfield in the thirties, the Okie kids would come to school, barefoot and tattered, but clean, for a glass of milk and leftovers.

We learned how important lunch was, especially if you didn't have any.

But back to lunch boxes. Inscribed in the sidewalk at 18th and Laurel in Pacific Grove are the names of Club Yellow, whatever that was. Of most interest was the name Lunchbox, along with Kate, and a few others. Who? What? Why? We'll never know.

Well, I'm sure there really are lunch provisions in those backpacks, all organic and nutritious. Not important locally, but I find you can indeed order bulletproof back packs. Knife proof, too.

*   *   *   *   *

Dress Right!

Back in the old days, between then and now, we used several stock market predictors, some more successful than others. The Super Bowl was one of the best, old NFL team wins, good market ahead. There was the Peruvian anchovy story, wheat blight someplace else in the world, some kind of Wave, sun spots, eclipses, not mention buyers versus sellers. The best, of course, was the mini skirt theory. The shorter the mini skirt, or dress, the higher the market. I guess you could also say, "More leg, more money!"

Time to check this out, I wandered up to Ocean Avenue to make notes, and friends, I hadn't realized how scarce are skirts, mini or otherwise, dresses or gowns. Ladies both young and not so young, are putting on their pants, as the saying goes, one leg at a time. Jeans, both loose and tight, pants, slacks, trousers, peddle pushers, and clam diggers, all well and good, but darned few skirts. Oh, there are the tennis outfits, but since those were always short, they aren't much use in determining a trend. I did notice some short shorts, which deserve further observation. Then there is the tightness of jeans factor, which may be promising, but also dangerous. OK, now this story is really more important for esthetics, rather than whether or not the market fluctuates in the right direction.

Look back in you old yearbooks, magazines and family photos, appreciate the lovely look of dresses, short or long. The girls walked with a sort of swing and style, impossible in blue jeans. I think. Remember the word "flounce?" The verb, not the noun. "She flounced down the street, as delightful as a summer breeze, her dress swinging just above her knees." There was Marilyn Monroe, over the air jet, and high school dances where the girls spun and twirled, with lovely legs revealed. Girls even wore dresses to The Boardwalk, pretending they didn't know about the air jets in The Fun House!

It is still entertaining to study the styles on Ocean Ave or Cannery Row and grudgingly appreciate those Calvin Kleins. A friend of mine who knows about such things claim that some strippers make an act of wriggling out their close cut Levis. Then for an encore, they wriggle them back on!

So ladies, for the sake of your country, or at least the stock market, take that rebate check and buy a dress – or skirt. Still discreet, but not too long.

I think I may have strayed from the subject, but in closing, "Never sell America short!" Or short short.

* * * * *

Easy Virtue, but Virtue Still

Every poker game the subject came up after a few hands and a couple of beers.

"Don't you wish that girls wanted sex as much as we do!"

Probably didn't use the word "sex," but the meaning was clear, and the conversation covered the same ground, the same theories, and misinformation from the week before.

And the rumor usually persisted about one girl or another who really did like to mess around in the back seat or the sand dunes or somebody's home.

This was rumor only since none of us poker players had actually, well, you know, done anything worth sharing, especially since gentlemen never told! (But always did.)

After a few more beers the fantasies got more lurid – walking barefoot across a field of breasts – being a male hooker – visiting a whore house in Watsonville, or even Tijuana! There always lurked the fear of VD with bizarre and horrible stories of marginal treatments and cures, not to mention possible pregnancy of Sally down the street.

Safety first, with a foil wrapped rubber in the wallet. Condom? What's a condom? Snickers about this falling out on the counter when you paid for the milkshakes or the cherry coke. Turned out that nobody had actually used one of these things, but just in case, and it was cautionary practice to put a new one in the wallet every two or three years. You could only imagine the trauma of actually buying a rubber at Dykes Drug Store, but luckily there was usually a vending machine outside the city limits.

It seemed, too, that we found out about potential, but lost opportunities just weeks after this Sally or that had moved away. "Yep," said the wise guys, "She really liked to do it!"

Wow! And we didn't know it! This one lovely had lived just across the street from me, a couple of years older, but always a sweet smile in my shy direction, and a throaty laugh when she walked off with girl friends. Tall, thin, willowy, I guess, with short black hair like Maria in "For Whom The Bell Tolls." She walked with a "what the hell" attitude, and I think went to school in Carmel, for some reason we never knew.

Just once that I'll never forget, she brushed into a party around a bonfire in the Sand Dunes – OK, a beer bust – and said "By God, my next door neighbor!" As I stood dumb and grinning, she kissed me, full out, and now sixty years later, I have almost recovered.

Well, think how things have changed, friends! Condoms in grammar school and very little left to the imagination. Open discussion on the school bus, and no need to drive to Watsonville, or so they tell me. And the mystery, ah, the mystery is still there! And guys still wish that girls wanted sex as much as they do!

* * * * *

Missing The Boat!

Flashing back to stories about the good old days, I'm reminded again that life without a few regrets and disappointments is life not fully lived. I think we all have had a few of both, some regrets things we did and some we didn't. I won't say that my dad was always chasing rainbows, but he did feel that he had missed a few opportunities. One miss that really stuck, wasn't his fault. Here it is.

In the mid or early 1920s, Dad in his late teens, living in Delano with his family, entered an essay contest sponsored by Zane Grey. Now if you haven't yet read, or have in dim recall, "Riders of The Purple Sage" and dozens of other stirring stories by ZG, hustle on down the library and make up for lost time. In the 1920s and 1930s Zane Grey was more popular than Hemingway, Steinbeck, and, all put together! The first writer, I think, to make a million bucks. For kid growing up in Delano, with all its charms, this was a big deal.

The subject of the essay was something like, "Why I Want To Sail To The South Pacific," and the prize was to sail with Zane Grey from LA or Long Beach, yep, to the South Pacific! At the time, my dad was contributing to the family income, driving a truck between Bakersfield and Los Angeles over the Grapevine. Even now that stretch of multi lane highway is no walk in the park, but imagine in the early twenties, hot, rough, plenty of boilovers and breakdowns, past those garden spots of Gorman and Castaic, but Dad dreamed of palm trees, glistening surf, lovely maidens, and felt pretty good about his chances. While he was away the telegram arrived in Delano. He had won and was told to report to the ship by a certain day and time!

His mother, my grandmother, concerned about any loss of income if my dad was sailing the seas, kept the telegram until after the ship had left. No second prize…. For a kid in the San Joaquin Valley in the 1920s, you can imagine his devastation. He recovered, met and married my mom in Pacific Grove, and lived happily ever after. The other great disappointment was the state track meet his senior year in high school. He normally ran the 100-yard dash in 10 flat, a good time in the old days. Day of the meet in Sacramento, hot and nervous, just before the race, he drank a Brown Cow! Otherwise known as a root beer float. Full and bloated, he came in second.

He was a great guy, a good father, a lot fun, and wonderful spinner of stories. He missed another boat or two along the way, but made as sure as he could, that his kids didn't. Miss the boat, that is. Well, maybe a few close calls!

* * * * *

Journalism 101

Flashing back on years of reading the Chron – still a decent newspaper, although not as good as it was when the Green Sheet was really green – it was those worldclass columnists that pulled me in every morning. We wouldn't dream of starting the day without Herb Caen! Hey, he might mention you or one of your friends, or even one of your enemies. The kid from Sakamenna warned us not to call our town Frisco, and in an ironic current twist of events, called it Baghdad By The Bay. He wrote with an off the cuff three dot style… breezy and brilliant, never over concerned with detailed accuracy. He was Mr. San Francisco… enjoyed poking fun at The Dreaded Piedmontese… of which I was one. He wrote with an eye and an ear from the Tenderloin to Pacific Heights, not universally loved, but always acknowledged. Spent a few years with the Examiner, but came back to the Chron where he really belonged. A classic.

But wait! There's more! Stanton Delaplane, Charles McCabe, and Art Hoppe! Impossible to pick a favorite, but these gentlemen should be required reading… that's what archives and libraries are for… in Journalism and English classes. I can't imagine them in E-mail, Facebook, or blogs, but then, I don't have to!

Stan Delaplane skipped from travel to local observations, with Postcards. His book on travels in Mexico is a classic. The 1961 Postcard from Monterey… judging Miss America and drinking martinis at Galatin's is a very fine historical piece! While a stickler for the truth, he also had a great imagination, beefing things up when necessary. Remember The Ding-Dong Daddy of the D Car Line? Among other things, his coverage of The State of Jefferson, northern counties that wanted to secede from California, got him the Pulitzer.

High in his obit is his intro of Irish Coffee to the Buena Vista, having first discovered this lovely lethal at the Shannon, Ireland, airport. Good story there! November 1952, he and the owner worked all afternoon perfecting the whipped cream float over the Irish whiskey. Almost passed out on the cable car tracks.

Charles McCabe, The Fearless Spectator! I would guess a third of his stuff comments on love/hate relationship with women, both in and out of marriage, and drinking in the many "watering holes" of North Beach. The titles of his book *Tall Girls Are Grateful*, and later, *The Good Man's Weakness*, give you a pretty good idea. His mother – also Irish – told him to always expect the worst, and he'd never be disappointed. He wrote about the damndest things, and made them interesting. If you can, dig out his story, The Fatal Glass of Beer. His most famous quote, "Any clod can have the facts, but having opinions is an art!"

The best of the bunch, in this tough crowd sprinkled with Pulizters, is Art Hoppe. He was a humorist, satirist, humanist, and journalist. His work is so good that it's tough to write about him without plagiarizing the praise in the Chronicle obit. You can look it up. More than an obit, really, a story of a great guy who happened to write. He could make you laugh or cry or shake your head and he told it like he saw it. "He deflated the pompous, tweaked the powerful and weighed in passionately on such issues as Vietnam, Watergate, the death penalty, and the inability of America to produce low-fat cheesecake." One of the chapters in his book, "Having a Wonderful Time, My First Fifty Years in the News Paper Business," said "Never Let Facts Get In the Way of a Good Story!" But even in his fables were great truths.

Well now, who's to take their place? Jerry? Erin? Joy? Jim? Royal? and one other that modesty prevents, but as Don Sherwood said every day, "Out of the mud grows the lotus!" You never know!

* * * * *

At Your Service!

Flashing back over the last half century, to the good old days and beyond, most of my blessed generation worked at one time or another in service jobs. Standing behind a counter, serving up soup, sitting with kids, pumping gas, delivering papers, we earned our four bits an hour, but more than that, we learned the value of service, and the attendant courtesy in dealing with people and to appreciate those people who serve and take care of us today. No point in further maligning the texting clerk or the I-Pod addict – they come in all ages – and they may never learn. But credit now those we take for granted, and sometimes don't even see.

As I mentioned before, I am blessed with health care people who are way above average, but you would never know it if their staffs weren't super efficient, kind, alert, and on the ball! Adding to the back office charm, of course, are those Docs whose wives take a very personal interest in a smooth running practice. Hey, my sister-in-law in Doctor Bowhay's office in Jackson, does a lot more than clean the parrot cages! There are ten of them.

You'll never know how fine a physician is if the faxes aren't sent, the phone not answered, or the appointments double booked. Give those gals – mostly gals – a thanks and a smile!

And Dr. Love wouldn't dream of looking at my teeth if Mary Berrey hadn't already cleaned them, and without Camille handing him the chisels, well you get the picture.

Think how irritated we'd be with Wells Fargo if that nice lady in front wasn't there to help us park. And even though we don't need help to our car from Safeway, how nice to be asked!

Some of the joy of our peninsula paradise comes from great places to eat, but if you had the best chef in the world – and we have several – you wouldn't know it if you were at the mercy of a snotty waiter.

A town is really defined by the people you see and are dependent on every day. Sure, the police, firemen, and the parking patrol, but what about Eric and crew who tunes up your car, or that lovely lady checking out books at the library, or those great guys who clean up the streets and carry away the trash! I know we all have green thumbs, but can you imagine the shambles of our town without those dedicated gardeners! Landscape experts.

I'm reminded of the buffalo that said, "I think I just heard a discouraging word," but that's what you'll never hear in Bruno's or Nielsen's! The Sutton's deserve a medal, or a least a big thanks for maintaining a good old fashioned grocery store, a family and Carmel tradition. It has felt comfortable, just walking down the aisles, and some of us even remember the Coke machine at the old place on Dolores.

Friends, I've jerked sodas, sold shoes, bellhopped, and a few dozen other things, and learned to accept a certain amount of abuse, but knowing that doing your job with a smile – OK, once in awhile not – gives a reward not counted on your W 2 at the end of the year. Yep, "Please" and "Thank you," heck, even "No problem," or "My pleasure," can really smooth the road. And isn't it great when a guest on our peninsula says "What nice, friendly people! They helped me find the way to the beach!"

When you visit Victoria in British Colombia you'll notice "Ambassadors" wearing special hats, there to serve, greet and guide the guests in town. Delightful! We don't need hats in Carmel. Just a big, welcoming smile!

• • • • •

For The Bible Tells Me So!

I guess I'm a hopeless fan of Country, Western, and Gospel and the other day stumbled on that Nick Sayers classic, "Jesus Loves Me, but He Can't Stand You!" If I was ever forced to preach a sermon – not likely – I think that would be my text. Now before I dip into this a little deeper, let me assure you that I don't believe that title, but that, spiritual friends, is the point.

Lately I move around between a church or two, looking for some of that old time religion I remember from the good old days in Pacific Grove. I grew up in the solid sanctuary of the Mayflower Congregational – now Presbyterian, but no matter – and was stunned returning home from college to find the family, Mom, Dad, sister and brothers, all Episcopalian. Now that may not seem like much of a shift to you, but good grief! Those Episcopalians all took communion right out of the same cup! Not only that, they read their prayers right out of a book!

Turns out my mother, Marilyn Bowhay, was the organist at St Johns for thirty eight years, apron strings, and all that. To top it off, my brother Mike is now an Anglican priest in Florida. Now Mike, in all fairness, is as open and broad minded, as say, a Pismo clam, but I am challenged when friends ask me which Anglican church? I won't dip into the slight difference between this and that, but I think you know what I mean. (Don't ever make a cute little joke about Catholic Light, or the differences between Catholic, Christian, Protestant, or Episcopal.)

Fellow English majors will remember that Jonathan Swift satire, "A Tale of a Tub," which suggests how we got to the current state of organized religion. It's a tough read, but glance at the Wikipedia summary. For more modern insights, read Philip Yancey's "Soul Survivor."

Growing up in God's Hometown, "Pacific Grove, by God," I remember friendly nods between the many congregations, but each of us were convinced that we had special insights into the Holy Spirit. Church camps at Mount Herman or Mount Toyon held us closer to the Lord than we ever have been since. To tell the truth, I don't think I ever heard "Conservative" or "Liberal" – maybe Fundamental – and the biggest question was "What about those unfortunates in some dark continent who never heard of Jesus? Would they go direct to Hell, without passing Go?" We agreed that Lutherans, Methodists, Presbyterians, Pentecostals, would all go to Heaven with the rest of us. Not too sure about the Mormons. And what about the Catholics? Sure were a lot of them, and they talked a lot about Confession, Purgatory and no meat on Friday!

Well, we've come a long way since Aimee Semple McPherson hid out in Carmel. The fire and brimstone of the good old days really paid off. Our faith is inclusive, and we respect a touch of dissent, but not too much.

What was that old hymn? Something about all being equal in His sight?

Yep, Moms and Pops, and those inbetween, and even those who aren't quite sure.

Jesus loves me, This I know, and I'm sure He at least likes you!

Amen!

* * * * *

Get Out The Vote, or Just Get Out!

Early now, in the political season, but even so, there doesn't seem to be much fervor, except of course, on CNN. A fair amount of inter party insults, but we can only hope that when we get down – or up – to Red vs Blue this passion will spread to we victims of the process.

Few will remember that cliffhanger in 1936, but boy, I sure do! Six years old, with the double whammy of being born into a Republican family and living in Bakersfield, I got the crap beat out of me for wearing an Alf Landon button to school. The button itself, was a thing of beauty, a blue center surrounded by a yellow fabric sunflower, but nevertheless, ripped from my sweater, and ground into the dust.

Washing my face and drying my tears, my parents explained to me the political process, freedom of speech, and something about the course of human events. And "Just wait! They'll sing a different tune in November!"

Of course Alf Landon lost to FDR by the biggest landslide in history, a record that stood until 1964 when LBJ knocked the socks off Goldwater.

Wearing my Rockefeller button to the end I escaped physical insult.

But back to Bakersfield. Our sixth grade teacher, with more fervor than sense, announced a debate, a debate, mind you, one side for FDR, and the other, for Wendell Willke! To pick sides, heads down, raise hands, and you know the rest. My Dad helped me write my argument, and a fine thing it was! Willke was one of us! He had worked in the fields of the Valley, still campaigned in shirt sleeves, and was not born with a silver spoon in his mouth, like that other guy!

Well, another show of hands, and it was something like twenty five to one. I sensed the mood of the class – a little late – and I knew that after the bell rang I'd get the crap beat out of me again. Sure enough.

The lesson of a bloody nose stays with you, and I have been relatively quiet – politically – since. Oh well, you remember the Truman/Dewey classic, and fortunately for me, we all liked Ike!

I plan to keep my mouth in check next year – a little old to get knocked down again – but, on the other hand, I have some valuable insights that I'll be happy to share, but not just yet!

* * * * *

Good Old Golden Rule Days!

Noticing kids walking down the hill from high school – Yep, Carmel, Monterey and Pacific Grove – I am reminded and remember that fine PG tradition of Hobo Day. We did our best to dress like hobos, sit in the sun, and take pictures. This wasn't much of a stretch for some of the gang, and this tradition must have survived to this very day. Maybe every day! This, of course, is good. "Hobo Chic" looks comfortable and is possibly good business for the thrift shops, and there is, I admit, something riveting about the bare midriff, I've even seen some mothers flaunting their belly buttons en route to Whole Foods! Witness then, a cell phone, and you suddenly feel very mature. Senior, in fact. Or old.

We did have other high school traditions in the good old days, in addition to serious study and prep for the future. Sadie Hawkins Day comes to mind, a tradition picked from Li'l Abner, a day and a dance when the gals were seriously empowered to ask the guys. If asked, it was very bad form to regret. Not too far from the Hobo Day décor, the gals dressed up like Sadie and Daisy Mae in Dog Patch style, long shirts tied in front, and pig tails tied in back. Somebody mentioned cleavage, a word we hadn't heard before, or a condition we hadn't noticed. "Like a what? A brick what!"

Filled with school pride, the Freshmen cleaned the year's weeds from the bleachers, with the upper classes cracking the whip, singing school songs. "The Red and Gold is in the Air" and Roll Breakers Roll! And what could be more memorable than a grand bonfire at the east end of the field, torched a night early by a graduated arsonist. Rebuilt by all of us the next day! Bigger and grander, with even a wrecked boat to top it off!

Not satisfied with just obeying the rules, we had Senior Ditch Day! After the 11:00 o'clock bell rang, the seniors marched off en masse (that's French) down Forest Ave to Lover's Point, with Mr. Cope in hot pursuit! Well, we milled around, sang a song or two, then marched back up Forest

Ave for afternoon classes. The senior boys were forced to sit out the next football game, but I don't think it mattered.

Who could imagine the talent, both raw and polished, in one high school!

The annual High Jinks showcased singers, dancers, musicians, comics, and actors! What a fine thing that that hallowed stage still features extraordinary talent.

Now it was one thing to have dances in the gym, every thing from sock hops to the May Dance. Good, rollicking fun, but maybe just a little bit restrained, or sterile. The real dances were at the Boy Scout Hall, known I guess, as Chautauqua, before and after the late forties. Didn't hear that in the good old days. But in addition to that venerable Troop 90, still in existence, it was the dances that set the stage. Parents or teachers or both watched carefully while we scattered dance wax, and played our 78s as loud as the equipment could handle. Crepe paper brightened the walls and you could almost hear the hormone level. A few smitten couples weaving to Glenn Miller in the center of the hall, and against the south wall, shy guys trying to get enough nerve to ask one of the gals – pretending boredom – against the north wall, to dance. Finally, just as Goodnight Sweetheart started, we bolted across the floor, said something inane, but we danced! It was a tradition.

I happened to glance in at a high school dance recently. What was this?

There was not a sound, but there were dozens of couples weaving around the floor in what I suppose, was rapture. Some fast, some slow, but dancing it was. I whispered to a chaperone and asked what was going on!

"Oh," she said. "They're all wearing I-Pods!"

* * * * *

Good Scents!

In flashing back I find I run short of memories, forgetting what I've forgotten about the good old days. Then I wander down to the beach, take a deep breath, and with just a whiff of rotting kelp, salty surf and cypress think, Gee! didn't the old place smell good! No, not just the sardines, but the pine needles, and the bay trees, and in the vacant lots, the wild fennel that reminded us of licorice. Whenever we got back from anywhere, that special Peninsula fragrance told us we were home. This all became more intense with fog on your face and in your hair.

The smell syndrome of course, includes other odors not quite as poetic; the rich pungent smell of tar when a new roof went up, and once in while somebody rode a horse through town and it was like a visit to a corral. I've talked about chicken coops before, and you might remember what it smelled like when you dipped the headless bird into hot water before plucking off the feathers.

Not many leaves to burn by the curb, but we did burn our trash in the back yard incinerator producing an acrid odor that alarmed the neighbors, but not for very long, and there was that good, healthy smoke from fireplaces and Franklin Stoves. And speaking of smoke, back in the good old days you remember we thought cigarette, pipe, and cigar smoke was good for you. Could smell it all over town. Smells awful today, but must admit, a whiff of Prince Albert, or God forbid, Lucky Strike does recall that first drag after a cup of coffee, or the lobby of the Forest Hill Hotel. No wonder our kids had asthma!

Homes, built a long time ago, had special individual vapors, almost like a fingerprint. Old wall paper, early brown Masonite, and vague reminders of something in the cooler that should have been tossed.

Our schools had their particular smells. Chalk dust, sweeping compound, pencil sharpeners, and erasers. On to high school, Arrid and Mum, Vitalis, Old Spice and Breck Shampoo lingering above impossible to conceal sweat, and even tears. The gym produced an organic combination of liniment and rotting socks but next door, the wholesome smell of sawdust from Wood Shop.

I dare you to notice a sweet scent of White Shoulders, My Sin, or Tabu, and not turn around to see if indeed she has come back, or maybe never left, and then close your eyes and drift back sixty years to the dance or the date, or even back to the locker next to yours.

Ah, Varian's Barber Shop! Bay rum, shaving soap, shoe polish and newspapers, all mixed together. Speaking of newspapers, The Tide, across from City Hall on Forest had that pleasant pungency of molten lead, ink and newsprint.

The beach had its own character with the briny wisps from the saltwater pool and some of the best hamburgers in the world cooking in the shed and across the street. Well, of course we sometime noticed the organic farewell of a sea lion. Still, today you can stroll up Eighteenth or Congress or Fountain around dinnertime and sniff the promise of a pie or cake or meatloaf!

Not to pass too quickly over Cannery Row and "The Smell of Prosperity", that was really our signature smell of The Peninsula in the good old days. When the wind was right they could even smell it in Carmel! The South end of Carmel Beach still has its unique reek! Sulphur spring, they say. Fisherman's Wharf was a heaven with steaming crab pots, frying fish, and from some place, a touch of creosote. Then up the hill with tamales cooking at The First Brick House.

Now, of course, the sad smell of smoke that reminds us of our fragile environment and what our friends and neighbors have lost.

Luckily there is a fine connection between our noses and the nostalgic part of our brains that takes us back to the good old days. Just step out down Forest, or out by Asilomar, and take a deep breath – best on a foggy night – and remember one more time, how lucky we all were! And still are!

PG Food... Before Julia!

Growing up in Pacific Grove I'm sure I never heard the word "Pagrovian," and I doubt if I ever heard "cuisine." But here I am, a Pagrovian, even though I live in Carmel, and I guess we had a cuisine in those days, but we called it something else....Like "food," or "dinner," or whatever, and we sure ate well. Then and now, food means love, and love means food, one way or another. There was, of course, plenty of love in old PG, but it seemed that all that food and love didn't run to overweight. I think that's because cholesterol hadn't been invented and we were urged to clean our plates, and eat good, square meals.

Remember, for instance, those hamburgers at Ruby's, down behind Holman's. They were served in a paper wrapper, settled in an aluminum cup. On the first bite, the fat just seemed to squirt out and drip down into the paper, down your chin and collect in the bottom of the cup. Best hamburgers then and since! Well, those at the beach shack were pretty good, too. Plenty of grease, a sloppy sauce, and salt air. The best we can do since then is In-N-Out and the best testament there are the hordes of folks buying the burgers, and I won't say the customers there are all heavy, but you'll notice none of them are skinny!

Realize, please, that "hamburgers" you get at Mission Ranch, Rustica, and a few other local restaurants are absolutely superb, rich and juicy, big enough to split with your sweetie and still have enough to take home for the dog. These, however, in my opinion, are not hamburgers in the old fashioned sense (just look at how much they cost!) but are really entrees. (There's another word I didn't hear in old PG).

Well, in that great stretch of years in the 19 s, forties, and even the fifties, food was simple, solid, basic, and good for you. Just look at us today! Well, that too, is another story. Dinner out meant Egg Foo Young at Tom's Café on Forest just across from Hellam's. There was abalone at Pop Ernst's and crab still warm from Liberty Fish and maybe roast beef, cooked to death, at the Forest Hill Hotel.

The real stuff, however, came from our Mom's kitchens and if you need a reminder, get a copy of Favorite Recipes, compiled by Ladies of the Mayflower Congregational Church. I'll let you borrow my copy. The advertisements alone will take you back to the <u>real</u> old fashioned days. Holman's, of course, Roy Wright Hardware, Fortier's Drug Store, Guy Getz Central Market, Dr. W. M. Gratiot, and Chas. K. Tuttle Established 1887, and many more, the fabric of our town.

But the recipes set the tone, mostly New England with a nod to the South, all straightforward and simple. Remember salmon wrapped in cheesecloth, boiled far too long, but saved by egg sauce? And aspic, found mostly at church potlucks. My mother's entry was Dundee Funk, which sounds more like a malady than a dinner, but there it was. Breads, cakes, pastries of all kinds have never been improved on, and if you don't believe me, try Mayonnaise Cake. Pickles, preserves, relish, dressings, and sauces, all carefully kept in the cooler. Find a nice old home in PG, still untouched, and in the cooler next to the kitchen I bet you'll find a jar or two of peach or plum preserves, "put up" seventy years ago. Don't touch.

Different homes were known for different things. I guess the Bowhay house was known for fried chicken, fried in lard, of course. The Tuck sisters did Tagliarini, a delicious casserole the color of their ancient wooden sink counter.

Mrs. Harris, with her family in the Holiday House, introduced me to Southwest Tostada. I've tried it all over the country since, and some of it close, but none as special as hers.

Just for memories sake I tried a can of Spam the other day. Yep, it still tastes the same. Mom dressed it up with brown sugar and cloves, served up with scalloped potatoes and sauerkraut. Right out of the can is OK, but use lots of very hot mustard.

* * * * *

Down to the Sea Again!

Growing up on the Peninsula, and I guess any place on the California coast, we were really part of the sea, and as I remember, we were more on the water than in it. Oh, we got wet when we needed to – launching a boat, digging a clam, getting an abalone, and once in awhile, just to show off, but for fun we did other things. The fact is that the water in our end of Monterey Bay was cold, and I mean really cold. You can check the records and find that wet suits didn't make the scene until the early fifties, and by that time most of us had our families started. Believe me, if we'd spent much time in the water before then, our families just might not have happened! The most beautiful piece of sand and sea is China Beach on Point Lobos, but if you think Lover's Point was cold, just dip your toe in the water and appreciate the fact that it's prettier than Waikiki!

The Pacific Grove saltwater plunge, modestly warmed, was filled in later for a beach volley ball set up. In the good old days, we paddled around, dived for dimes, and cannon balled off the board. I suppose we did that dumb Marco Polo thing, too. We did learn to swim there, shivering at 7: in the morning. We threatened to swim in the pool just long enough to get ready, then race down to the sand, swim very fast and out, on to the beach or into the showers. Yep, we threatened, but very seldom pulled it off. My sister, Shirley, only slightly nuts, never seemed to mind the icy chill and was known to swim all the way out and around to the Point. Happily, she lived later and swam off Waikiki, now frolics in the surf where she lives in Savannah. In between, she was a Feast of Lanterns princess.

There was, of course, peril in the ocean, and December 7, 1952, Barry Wilson, a junior at PGHS, was surfing just off Lover's Point, and was killed by a Great White. A few months later a swimmer was bitten on his heel by a sea lion. A few more, over the years, and we realized that the ocean was not totally ours.

The world's best biology teacher, Ferdinand Ruth, waded around the tide pools with us, pointing out chiton, anemones, and hermit crabs, warning us to never turn our back on the ocean. Lord love the curious, and one kid stuck his tongue – no, I couldn't make this up – on an open anemone, and he damn near died on the spot. Tongue swelled up, and all that. He lived and decided to move to Kansas.

We've talked about this before, but you really had to love abalone, 5:00 in the morning, extreme minus tide, wade out in your tennis shoes and levis, up to your waist, to put it politely, reach under a rock covered with eel grass, and hope to find an ab before being bitten by a Moray Eel. Having turned your back on the ocean a semi surf knocked you on your butt, and so much for the warm sweat shirt. But by golly, back to the house, and the thrill of it all, cleaning those big reds, slicing the steaks, pounding just right, and then a perfect platter, fit for the Gods! Too bad I hadn't then learned about Chardonnay. Denise Williams, who wrote that lovely Laurel, remembers her dad pounding on the back porch, and bemoans the fact that abs are no longer free. Oh, what the hell, Denise, buy a few on Wharf Two! Small, expensive and almost as good as we remember. and the "recession" is practically over!

* * * * *

Waltz Me Around Again, Willie!

Here we are again, into Prom Season! Ah, we old grizzled and disillusioned, take a moment, look back, close your eyes, open your hearts, and remember the thrill of it all! Starting right after Christmas, and maybe earlier, the plans were started. First, who to take or be with, and the gals, what to wear. Some moms started sewing, something new, or thirty years old, with fresh lace or satin bows. "No, Mom." She said. "It's nice, but I rather have something new from Holman's! I'll baby sit and earn the money!"

The boys, suddenly young men, worried more about who to ask than what to wear, but that came later.

I thought that corsages might have faded from practice, along with other things, but local florists tell me the corsage market is alive and well, more toward rose buds, but good old gardenias still hang in there. And boutonnieres! Carnations still.

Some parents, attempting to save us all a buck or two, constructed little bouquets from the garden, but those usually wound up in a cheese glass on the kitchen sink. The most sensible arrangement was the wrist corsage, still a favorite, but as the ladies arm was raised to the gent's shoulders, some sneezes tainted the moment. Some lucky gals wore leis, fresh from Honolulu, expense be damned. Home made leis of nasturtiums proved unsatisfactory. Here and there, a rose or orchid in the hair had a dramatic overtone. The problem with the regular corsage was where to hang it. The long, formidable pins were dangerous, and blood on the bodice could spoil a whole evening. Moms usually said something like, "How lovely, Roger! Sally, lets go in the other room and I'll pin it!"

Now even in those days, good old, as they were, some gals did wear the bare shoulder variety of gown. Accidents were not common, but they did happen. My granddaughters tell me that there have been great engineering advances since the 1940s. But gravity is tough – after all it's the law – and bouncing around with a pound of gardenias above the breast did create problems. Some gals did have a higher center of gravity than some of their classmates, and this did help the off the shoulder circumstance.

Time to recall that great Doris Day scene. "What God has forgotten, we stuff with cotton," and her mother dusted off two powder puffs, one for each, as it were. Lovely to look at, but at the dance, at least one fell to the floor! Worth seeing "On Moonlight Bay" again.

The Senior Prom was usually the first time a guy got dressed in formal wear. You know, a tux! Out of the mothballs, came all sorts of rigs that Uncle Charley work fifty years ago. Vests, cumberbunds, high stiff wing collars, and all sorts of jackets. About half were in white dinner jackets, but every outfit was different. Bow ties, clipped on or tied. Fifty different styles, and not a moth to be seen.

Moms and Dads nervously chaperoned, poured the punch, and watched the door. Phonograph records, all year, but tonight, Hank Springer and his Rhythm Six on the gym stage, good old dance wax from one free throw line to the other.

Not much trauma on the floor. After all, once in a lifetime, and all that, but earlier in the evening all Hell broke loose when Dad said, "I'll drive and you two can sit in the back seat.

"What!" came the scream! "I can drive! I've got my license!, and we had planned to double date with Jim and Judy!"

I don't remember who won way back then, but twenty-five years later my son got to drive. After all, he had washed the car, not to mention rented a tux.

• • • • •

Music!

How lucky we are to live in the Music Capitol of The World! Yep, the Monterey Peninsula, home of hymns, harmony, Rock and Roll, Classical Class, and everything in between. Bach, Boogie, Jazz and Blues and while we are blessed with "Festivals" almost every week, there's plenty of toe tapping, hip swaying, jumpin' jive on those "off" nights. OK, so it's sometimes a little pricey at Golden State and Sunset Center, but remember those good old words to live by, "Quality is remembered long after price has been forgotten." You'll remember that Bach Mass long after you have forgotten how much the ticket cost, and how much did I pay to hear Willie Nelson?

But no matter, most music is free anyway! Have a glass of wine at Mission Ranch some night and hear and watch "The Russian" play the piano. (His name really is Gennady Loktionov, but "The Russian" is easier.)

And there's no cover at Hyatt, fourth Sunday afternoons for the best jam session in the country. Only polite to buy a glass of wine, or bring your banjo and jump right in! Deep trouble to mention only a few other local treasures by name, but when you get Dave Morwood, Lee Durley, Jim Vanderzwan and couple of lovely Canaries* in front of the bass and hot guitar, you'll wish Mom had make you practice more!

Music and nostalgia are really the same, and remember in the good old days the great bands and artists that did the Soldier's Club at Fort Ord! Big bands galore and Stan Kenton doing Tampico! And the celebs at the Crosby! Once upon a time, the 1940s, some of us hitched a ride to Salinas, and there in the high school gym, on stage, just two of them, Louis Armstrong and Jack Teagarden! Satchmo, with a stack of handkerchiefs on a piano, wiped his brow and his lips, trumpet and trombone pumped our pulses for hours on end. I think three couples danced in back of gym, but the rest of us crowded and deep in front of the stage. I think it cost a buck, but worth every dime!

With all that music in the air we were swept to form our own bands. Monterey High kids had a jazz quintet that played for us at a PG High assembly, so good we almost became Toreadors! Six of us put together a group, playing at the Pacific Grove Rec Center, led by George Mattos of Pole Vault fame who was even better than Benny Goodman on the clarinet. They tried me out on the piano, but I was slow at reading music and was always about three measures behind, still playing while the rest went out for a Coke. They suggested maybe I should start a few minutes and measures early, but success there was limited. I was switched to the drums and Johnny Price played the piano. He was good and went on to piano fame in San Francisco. George Mattos still plays the clarinet, runs a Dixieland bunch in Ashland, having finished a music professor career at College of The Siskiyous.

KRML and KIDD do their best to take us back and if you're lucky you'll hear Erroll Garner's Concert By The Sea, and the original Misty. Carmel stuff! And the price is right as you wander down Alvarado and wind up on Cannery Row. Music all around! What a great place to live!

So, Put Another Nickle In The Nickleodian.....and you know the rest.

*Canary. A possibly forgotten term used to describe lovely lady singers, usually found in front of a band. Not to be confused with "cannery."

* * * * *

How to Save Pacific Grove! (*maybe*)

Two momentous things happened in 1950. First, I was readmitted to the University of New Mexico, having flunked out in glorious disgrace a year earlier. Second, the town of Hot Springs, New Mexico, changed its name to Truth or Consequences. You could look it up!

It's quite a story, but in 1950 the most popular TV game show, Truth or Consequences, was hosted by master showman, Ralph Edwards. He promised to broadcast the show from the first town to change its name. Yep, Hot Springs won, and its been Truth of Consequences ever since. Fame, fortune, and a nice place to stop between Albuquerque and El Paso. Now called T or C by the locals, they never looked back.

I'm reminded of sports venues with recent renaming deals. I thought it silly at first....Qualcomm, Petco, Nike...but realizing this made big bucks for all concerned, my thoughts turn to good old Pacific Grove. OK, the last hometown is a jewel with nothing like it anywhere else in the world. Nice, cute, quaint, solid, breathtaking and beautiful....but broke! Or so it seems to be when we read about potential shut downs, or shut ups, of the library, museum, police and fire, City Hall, and good grief, the golf course!

Now how about this. PG contacts Disney...that's right, Disney. Proposes a deal, for a million a year, next ten years, we name the town Disneyville! Might even make it Disneyville/PG, or Disneyville/Pacific Grove, but you get the picture! No mouse parades, no theme rides, no fireworks. Just the solid self-confidence of Pagrovians Forever!

OK...So Disney says there's a waiting list. We contact Harris Ranch!

* * * * *

I Love a Parade!

I guess every season is a parade season, and there is always something about parades that thrills us, pulls us to stand on the curb, looking down the street..."Here they come! Here they come!" All the towns in the county have at least two or three a year, themed with everything from artichokes and butterflies to history icons or holy pageants from "the old country."

We are multi blessed here in God's Country with car after car after car, roaring or muttering down the avenues. And where do they get all those blonde beauties sitting next to the drivers, hair blowing in the wind! Must come with the entrance fee.

Pacific Grove, being "The Last Hometown," was made for parades with the heart thumping combination of patriots, military, Monarchs, families and kids. Pine Avenue, from Washington Park to Robert Down is the perfect parade route, wide enough for motorcycles, marching bands, and a horse or two, all at the same time. This year's pageant was perfect, and if you haven't seen the bulldog on the skateboard, you haven't been to enough parades.

You need a couple of marching bands to really set the tone, and when you hear "Sound Off," with the drums responding "Ruff ruff! Ruff ruff! RRRR, Ruff Ruff," then the first clear notes from the trumpets and trombones, it's hard to keep from stepping out and marching along! And then, friends, along comes an Army, Navy, or Marine drill team and you wish you could run downtown to buy war bonds. (Really, peace bonds.) and for the moment, you're glad you pay income tax! Almost.

But it's the kids that really make a parade. Not soul stirring, maybe, but parents delight, as little Sammy or Sally pull their wagon, with red, white and blue bunting, and a suffering dog or cat, in costume for the occasion, either pulled along or tied in the wagon or buggy.

Of course you can't have a real parade without kids tossing candy to the crowd. A few fights in the gutter, but that's all part of the fun. In the old days we thought maybe too many horses, and today it might be too many cars. Well, cars don't crap, and no exhaust fumes from the old gray mare, so it all evens out. And look! Look! Look at those ladies on stilts1 Must be twenty feet up, and look! They're dancing! And look at that sweet little butterfly outfit!~ She can't be more than two!

OK. Remember that 1946 Fourth of July parade in Monterey? If you don't, check the Internet and see the First Theatre float. And tell me why girls of Italian descent look so beautiful in white gowns with mantillas over that stunning black hair, especially in a parade! Well, I'm starting to drift.

But one more thing. When I was kid in Bakersfield my Uncle Harold was Kern County Fire Chief and drove an open Buick convertible in the Pioneer Day Parade. And there, my wildest dream fulfilled, I sat next to him and waved at the crowd. After five blocks I as totally bored, and realized that when you're in a parade, all you see is people. The moral of the story.... It's sometimes better to stand on the curb and watch the parade, then actually be in it. Words to live by.

"Look! Look! Here they come!"

*   *   *   *   *

Articles of Lasting Interest

I haven't done my usual research on the subject, but I'm willing to bet that most of the homes on the Monterey Peninsula built before 1910 have storerooms. Yep, that's what they were called. Storerooms, and if you can find a few that have not been pilfered or pruned, my what treasures you'll find!

Among old lightning rods and buggy whips, Uncle Sumner's shaving mug, Mason jars, both empty and filled, you might find that steamer trunk, not opened for a hundred years. Some day I'll tell you about the Radium Revigator, but that's another story.

What I really want to get into here, next to the stacks of National Geographic's, are those dozens of Reader's Digests! Presently, their slogan is AMERICA IN YOUR POCKET, worthy enough, but in the 30s and 40s, it might have been The World By Your Bedside! The current publication is all well and good, but like so many things, it was better then, right next to The Weekly Reader. No advertisements and plenty of great condensed books, and the teachers didn't mind if we used them for book reports. The articles really did open the world, and after all, there was no TV, so you had to read if you wanted to learn anything.

Remember that great piece on how to be totally self sufficient on an acre or two of land? Your own chickens, rabbits, a goat or a cow, and the manure nourished the vegetable garden, and mulch and all that. Turned out to be somebody's imagination and it just didn't work, but what fun to dream about! And the couple that emptied their piggy bank each year, went to Greyhound, said they had thirty-seven dollars, or whatever, and asked how far they could go. They'd hop off to some little known town where they had never been and have a delightful vacation. For a kid in Pacific Grove that sounded like a very creative adventure.

During the early forties, at least half of the stories talked about the war, heroes, victory, and the need for sacrifice. "Here's Why There's

Nothing to Spread on Your Bread.," "The Navy Fliers Dish it Out," and "Colonel Carlson and His Gung Ho Raiders." "This Is Your Blood in Action."

OK, so it was a different war…

We have forgotten the "Most Unforgettable Characters", but we still have "Life in These United States." A quick review features some stereo-types we wouldn't call political correct today, but there was plenty of spiritual inspiration. "There Are No Atheists In the Skies," or in foxholes.

There was always a good dose of health advice and education. Something like "I Am Joe's Liver" or "I Am Joe's Heart." This was war time, of course, and mothers were admonished to keep close eye on their daughters. There was concern on the spread of what we call today STDs, but Reader's Digest laid it right out there. Venereal disease, and the scourge of syphilis! Good news, though, from Paul de Kruif…."Stamping Out Syphilis With a One Day Treatment." All this still strong enough to severely limit physical contact.

Well, dig out a copy or two from the store room. The jokes are old enough to recycle, the insights timeless – sort of – and you can dig up plenty of trivia to amaze your friends at The Carmel Foundation!

And yes, just above the Contents, it promised, Articles of Lasting Interest!

* * * * *

Innocence

I remember hearing that pure innocence starts downhill as soon as a baby is born. Pure, clean and without sin, or experience, for that matter, and that exposure to life taints the soul. Conscience enters the picture sooner or later and somewhere we learn right from wrong. Overlooking the "the terrible twos" I don't think modest badness starts until around kindergarten, but on into grammar school, we learn, observe, imitate and get some bad habits.

Getting into the teen years we learn and yearn and discover, gradually, lust.

It is no mean trick to get out of high school innocent and pure, fantasies not withstanding. I was saved from indiscretions – well, most indiscretions – by passionate restraint, or perhaps, restrained passion, never again with a conscience so clean. Some kids smoked and some kids drank and some messed around in the back seats of cars, but Lord, not me! Not me! I was an athlete!

But then, with a glorious shout, off to college! It took some time to shake off the Puritan ethic of Pacific Grove – two or three weeks – and truth be known in that summer between high school and college I at least became aware of carnal possibilities.

Look now, at the current crop of potential sinners. I mean teenagers. They do things, which seem to be accepted, and often approved. Of course, they are all going straight to Hell, but then, maybe not! They are missing that delicious feeling of guilt, that guilt we felt in the good old days. Knowing that you had stepped over the line – just a little bit – and gotten away with it, did wonders for private self-esteem. After all, not sure if it's mentioned in the Bible, but self-righteousness is a sin in itself.

But now, these many years and many sins later, look back and cherish that sweetness of senior high school love. If we look closely, without snap judgment, we may notice a couple of high school kids – boys and girls –

strolling hand in hand, swinging down the lane, love light in their eyes, still almost as innocent as kindergarten, not knowing, that next year will be even better!

*   *   *   *   *

Forbidden Fruit

I tread lightly here, on the edge of political or social correctness, but I would be false to our memories if I left out any discussion of a few baskets of forbidden fruit. The despair, for instance, of my Catholic pals, Jerry, Len, Jim, and others in the strictures of The Index! As we understood it, The Index came from The Vatican, no less, and listed the books forbidden by God. We can only guess that this had something to do with variations on the reproductive process, or certain parts of the human body, and might even noted a movie or two. Fortunately, my friends were able to confess any glimpse at titillating material and so avoided the need for further physical education in the back row of The Grove Theatre. The power of the printed word and the need for knowledge would not be denied, however, and The Index was abolished in 1966.

Back in the good old days, even Protestant parents had their own sort of index with certain types of reference material hidden in the back of a dresser drawer. Some libertine families, possibly military, kept these books right out in the open, although on the top shelf of the bookcase. On inspection these books would flop right open to the important pages. It did take a certain amount of seeking through Boccaccio's Decameron, but sooner or later, there it was. No need to struggle with Henry Miller who was an easy reference. That First Theatre classic, In The Bushes At The Bottom Of The Garden, might well have fostered further interest in Lady Chatterley.

What a gal!

The scattered censorship of The Memoirs of Hecate County by Edmund Wilson, triggered an enthusiastic search for the book, at least, by me. And there it was, on a top shelf behind the desk, in the library of God's Hometown, Pacific Grove! Claiming journalistic license, I took the book home and went to work. Believe me, friends, it wasn't worth it. Tedious, tiresome, and boring – oh sure, well written – it added little to the seduction of the reading public. To check my memory, I borrowed the book last week from the Carmel Library, and found it even more tedious than it was back in the good old days. After wading through several hundred pages I found an included commentary by John Updike, an expert on such things, and he noted the exact pages, those kernels of knowledge, that caused the uproar.

Take my word for it. Buy instead a copy of Playboy.

Recalling Forever Amber and the revelations of Peyton Place I'm trying to construct a steamy story about Pacific Grove in the good old days. Might have to work on Carmel instead.

This whole subject caught my attention when I heard the *The Joy of Sex* has been reissued in a revised edition! Revised! Good grief! Have we been doing it wrong?

* * * * *

Button Up Your Overcoat!

I'll have to ask Marty Larkin when central heating, like forced air, came into Pacific Grove, but I know for sure it wasn't around at 18th and Laurel in the 1940s. This came to mind this past week as Indian Summer passed in to winter. I know, I know. Nothing like Minnesota, but baby, it was chilly! Out to get the paper was a challenge, but back in the house, a tweak of the thermostat, and our living room was almost like May in Maui.

Back in the good old days somebody had to be the first on the floor to light the heater in the living room, twist on the floor furnace in the dining room, or struggle lighting pinecones in the Franklin Stove. The whole thing really pulled the family together, once in the kitchen, as we huddled around the open oven door. Bad idea, but widely practiced. Up in the bathroom we had a very old electric heater that glowed bright red for a moment before it blew out a fuse. Remember fuses?

The house was very lonely on those 4:30 mornings when I shivered into the kitchen, warmed up Ovaltine or Postum, and then pedaled away on my old Schwinn to deliver papers. For some reason it never seemed as cold on those mornings up early to fish. If you got up early enough and are now old enough you might remember the incinerator pit behind the grammar school where we paper boys gathered to warm our hands.

Even after most of the town had refrigerators – Fridgidaires – we kept our ice boxes, the Union Ice man with those big heavy tongs, carrying ice up the back steps, even on the coldest days. In the Navy I learned about the "free surface effect." which explained why the water under the icebox always spilled, en route to the set tubs.

You'll remember, of course, that almost every house on the Peninsula had a "cooler" in the kitchen, a cupboard so constructed that through a screened opening the sea breezes cooled the contents, everything from pies, pickles, cheese, butter and jam. We were way ahead, and early on that "green" stuff!

Some items got shoved to the back, forlorn and forgotten, and when rediscovered months or years later the interesting variety of molds solved the mystery of those strange odors we had noticed! Once upon a time I yearned to learn taxidermy and as interest faded, I left the skin of some creature in the cooler, discovered by Mom years after I had left for college. Along with five years of Monterey Jack it wound up in the land fill, but still "organic!"

There are advantages in our semi cool climate. Good for the skin, and I guess our souls. I told a friend in Chicago today that it was so chilly we had to leave the heat on last night. Somehow the connection got lost. Like the time last summer when I told a cousin in Bakersfield that we had a real heat wave here in Carmel. Got up close to seventy! She hung up, too.

* * * * *

Letters

Looking for an old yearbook in the basement trunk I uncovered an old shoe box, left there years ago. I smiled to myself – nobody there to see me – and realized that I had uncovered a treasure, long forgotten, but put there over sixty years ago. Love letters from the girl in Indianapolis! It's a long story. More about that later.

But flashing back, I realized how things are different now. Not better or worse, but different. Each year now, more and more holiday cards on the Internet. Clever, funny, most now with music, and certainly sincere. Some of us still send cards and letters in the mail, even though we might have to type out the words on Word, but most of the correspondence now comes E-mail, Twitter, Facebook or Texting, whatever that is. All great stuff with lots of advantages, not to mention reconnecting with people you'd rather forget. But then, by Golly, you hear from sweet Sally or good old Richard the Rascal, long ago drifted away by circumstance.

As I opened the shoebox I expected – and hoped – to get a breath of perfume dripped on the paper a long time ago. No luck, but look! The stamps, those old red airmails, stuck on upside down. Remember? Meant love, or at least deep affection.

And there, too, SWAK, and other initials, meaning long forgotten. I brush my fingers across that lipstick kiss and think how tough to send that on the Internet. I remember standing by the mail slot in the front door, then ran upstairs with the envelope. This was important since, as you well remember, mothers, bless their hearts, were expert at steaming open envelopes.

That skill has faded away since mothers, bless their hearts, are able to do a little secret surveillance on the computer.

Now friends, one of the good things about old letters, love or not, is that once in the shoebox, they're private! Not so with E-mail, as many a wanderer has recently discovered.

In the good old days, sure, you could make a long distance phone call, but it cost a week's work and there was always little sister, brother, or Mom, on the other side of the door. Now, of course, the kids step outside with their cell phone and murmur away. I think in the good old days, distance really was a blessing, and sooner or later, local honeys settled happily into our lives with one last letter across country, "I really do love you... Sincerely, ..."

A whole different thing when you were far, far away in the service. "Mail call, Mail call," the bos'n piped, and we hurried to the wardroom. We put those letters from our wives and sweethearts under our pillows, read them over and over, studied the photographs, and agonized over the rumor that our deployment would be extended. Those letters are in a separate shoebox. Well, hooray for the Internet, but grandkids, give it one more try. Send a letter! Support the Government! Buy a stamp!

*   *   *   *   *

The *Real* Fishermen's Wharves

Lots of reasons to wander out on Monterey Wharf #2. LuLu's where we used to buy bait and now get good calamari. No connection! Then Sand Bar with sand dabs about as good as you can get, and out near the end, Royal Seafood and you can't get fresher fish anywhere. OK, some close, but Royal – not related to Royal Calkins – just feels like fish. Smells just right, too.

The boats still tie up along side, and yesterday the boys were mending nets on the wharf. In the old days they mended nets in the field just above and across from Tarpy's. That's why it's called Fisherman's Flat. Figures.

In the good old days fishing off the wharf was potluck and we happily caught mackerel, smelt, perch, and even a salmon or two. The mackerel runs were legendary, with millions of fish swirling both sides of the wharf, no bait necessary. Bare hooks worked just fine, and some of the windows on the east side were shattered as we horsed in the fish, swinging them over our heads. This all before I realized how good mackerel is to eat – if cooked right – but they sure helped the roses grow! One fish per bush.

And boy, the crab! We'd drop out nets over the side, baited with a fish head or two, wait ten minutes, then lift up the loot.

When we were kids living in Bakersfield, brother Brooks suffered bad, bad with asthma. Driving up to the Peninsula, first stop was the wharf. Brooks, maybe eight years old, walked to the very end, stood and breathed for almost an hour. It became part of his soul, and yep, Brooks became Monterey's first Harbor Master. More about that some other time.

In those good old days the harbor was alive with activity, boats coming and going with whistles and horns. The boats were mostly working boats, supplying the canneries with sardines. The purse seiners were the most beautiful things afloat, or so it seemed at the time. Tom Aliotti owned and captained the California Star, strictly a sardine boat, in and out of Monterey. During the war – WW2 – the Navy took it over as a patrol vessel in South America. After the war Tom got the Star back, rebuilt and fished it for a couple of years, then sold it. It was part of a fleet destined for Formosa's fishing industry, but went down in a typhoon, all hands lost. Tom, now 94, was the classic fisherman, working at one time or another from the Bering Sea to South America, cruised up and down the coast, but Monterey was home, between Fisherman's Wharf and Wharf Number 2.

These were the guys that inspired Armin Hansen, and shame on you if you haven't seen his work at La Mirada. There are beautiful models of the commercial boats, along with lots more of our heritage in the Maritime Museum.

There used to be a fine "secret" clam bed right next to Pop Ernst's, just below the monkey grinder. After the clams discovered that lead batteries had been dumped in the harbor – since removed – they left, or so the story goes. Way, way back in the forties, standing on the end of Wharf 2, you could hear the thump, thump, thump of ladies pounding abalone in the packing shed across the harbor.

There are dozens of wonderful books and articles about our Harbor, but don't be satisfied just reading. Take a walk out on either wharf – or both – and breath that air, both fresh and pungent. It's best early morning. Close your eyes and listen to the sounds still there. Just don't step off the end!

* * * * *

No Friend Like An Old Friend

Flashing back through some old Peanuts' files, Linus and his security blanket took me back to the good old days when my kids had their own blankies. Usually old blankets, but sooner or later, shreds of cloth, held close to the face and up to the ear, other hand with a thumb in the mouth. Here I am now, seriously mature, and wonder how much better I'd be today if I'd kept mine. Actually, my talisman was a stuffed dog, looked like an Airdale, and I think smelled like one, too. Turns out these favorite rags, teddy bears or dolls were probably germ nurseries, but woe to the mom or dad who dared to wash them!

Once you reach the age of reason I think a teddy bear is more socially acceptable than faded flannel. And yes, lots of people, well adjusted, keep these companions forever and ever. A friend of mine, well into his sixties, had a Pooh Bear, about six inches tall, complete with hat. He couldn't sleep at night unless this little baby was on his night stand. Many years ago now, Herman and his wife drove from Paris, well into Provence, and then realized that Pooh had been left in the hotel. Now you or I might have said "Too bad," and maybe bought another bear, but long drive or not, back to Paris they drove, found Pooh on the concierge desk. With tears in his eyes, Herman apologized – to the bear – and they lived happily ever after.

This not quite the same as the lady at a table next to us, upstairs at Chez Panisse. She sat her bear, dressed in a sailor suit, in a high chair, ordered lunch herself and for Roger. Roger didn't eat his lunch. Mom said he wasn't hungry. The waiter didn't even blink. Berkeley, after all.

Susie's grandson, Zachary, nicknamed Zee, had a nice, white chenille friend he called Herezee. That since his parents, when he was a baby, would hand this to him, saying "Here, Zee!" Get the connection?

Turns out kids can't be fooled, or tricked into taking new blankies into their souls. Parents have tried to substitute lost rabbits or rag dolls, but it's a wise kid who knows his own blankie.

I know that some people will carry a rabbit's foot until Kingdom Come, and that's not quite the same…like a St Francis on the dash board. No, a real teddy bear, or Snoopy, or Little LuLu is a real friend you can talk too, cry with, or even take the place of a Kleenex if you have a runny nose. Nothing on the Internet surprises me any more, but Wow! Log on to Teddy Bear and discover that you are not alone in your attachment to little old Smoky.

Barbie dolls and Ken have a certain fan base, but these are collectibles, pride of ownership and all that, but I doubt if they enjoy emotional attachment. OK! OK!, maybe I'm wrong, but for a kid's first Christmas, a nice fuzzy, furry whatever will be a friend forever! Might give one to the parents, too!

* * * * *

Open Wide!

If you've had any dental work lately – you know, fillings, root canal, crowns, and all that – you realize that it doesn't hurt any more. Well, maybe a little, but sure not like in the good old days! In Pacific Grove we were blessed with the oldest practicing dentist in the state of California. Maybe in the whole country, but nobody checked. I don't know how old was Dr. Jarvis Williams when he pulled his last tooth, but he was sure old enough to tell you about the early days of the Monterey Peninsula – the very early days.

He was a delightful gentleman, lived across the street at Eighteenth and Laurel, with a nice lawn and oak trees. Gone now, of course. Both.

Every day he walked to his office above Dyke's Grove Pharmacy, his waiting room now where A J rubs everybody the right way. He wore a grey fedora and dark blue serge three piece suit and in the office, tossed the hat on a rack along with his coat, and got to work still in his vest and necktie. He tied a napkin around the neck of the suffering souls, handed them a cup to spit in, and said "Open wide!"

His office smelled like a dentist's office, a mixture of wintergreen and cinnamon, and smack in the middle, the chair with the promise of pain and agony. In later years I claimed that novocaine had not yet been discovered, then learned that it had been around for a long time, but was expensive, and after all we were only kids! Well, I won't dwell here on the drill, driven by the foot activated motor, pulleys and strings, slow and fast, deep and devastating. Then, after twenty-seven hours of cavity destruction, a rest while he hummed and shaped the stuff to fill the hole. The best was yet to come and as we waited for whatever it was to set or cure, Dr. Williams sat at his desk, even more cluttered than mine today, and played the clarinet!

Well, sooner or later my folks noticed some decline in the hand/eye coordination and we took our teeth to Dr. Damson in Monterey. (Not his real name.) He did, indeed use novocaine and as far as I remember, he did not play a musical instrument. He was much admired by my Dad as a man of the world in addition to being a damned fine dentist. Maybe apocryphal – and the best stories usually are – but the story was that each year he spent a two week vacation on Howard Street, in San Francisco. In case you don't remember, that was Skid Row, and then some. The good dentist wore his oldest clothes, tattered and torn, didn't shave, took no money, and hung out with the bums and broads, taking nourishment out of a paper bag with the rest of them. Back to the office in two weeks, showered, shaved, and loaded with new stories to tell between drills.

Now look around you today at those spiffy, sanitary dental offices, without a drill in sight. Nice KBOQ classical music, and no need for a clarinet. Yes, a tiny stick as the lidocaine slips in, and then a magic laser, washed with cool jets from the hand of a lovely assistant, removes the bad stuff, in goes the new, and $1500 later you wonder how soon you can come back.

* * * * *

Home Base

Now when we travel hither and yon, whether to Modesto, Boston, or Barcelona and mention our hometown on the Monterey Peninsula, the first icon to come up is, of course, Clint Eastwood. Not so in the good old days when Clint was still in high school. Flashing back, our landmarks were Fort Ord, Cannery Row, John Steinbeck, and as Golf Capital of the World, Pebble Beach! The title "Del Monte" rang loud and true, and we called the gated forest The Drive, as in Seventeen Mile. Now my memory is as good or bad as yours, but I think "Pebble Beach" meant just the golf course. The lodge was The Lodge, MPCC was "The Club," and Cypress Point, just that.

Cypress famous since we all knew Henry Puget, the head pro, and his beautiful daughter, Yvonne, PGHS 1949. Henry's older brother, Cam, was the pro at Pebble and later at The Club. Cypress now still famous since our classmate, Marty Larkin, PGHS 1947, is still a working caddie!

You would think, growing up in PG I would have become a real golfer. The Fred X. Fry dynasty who ran that great 9 hole number in Pacific Grove did their best, but I was off to something else, I'm not sure what.

Dropping a name, my close friend Sam Lindamood, pastor at Piedmont Community, said Bowhay, you may play golf, but you'll never be a golfer!

A compliment, perhaps. And oh yeah. Sam was the third to ever hole in one the 16th at Cypress. You could look it up!

As kids, we picnicked at Indian Village, stood under the Lone Cypress, admired the Ghost and Witch Trees, and rode our bikes around Point Joe. Yep, we had Lake Majella, right behind the Sand Plant, sort of a swampy mess, but with great frogs.

As the sand dunes were munched away during WW2, we guessed that the sand revenue kept Del Monte afloat during the war. There was some pride and consolation thinking that the world's purest sand made binoculars and bomb sites. And then too, our sand made Waikiki famous.

Remember the excitement when a glass bottle was found at Fan Shell Beach, right near Bird Rock! Curled inside, a lead sheet noting that Sir Francis Drake had paused here on his way North. Mid forties, I think, and you can check the archives. Or maybe I should.

Best of all, we now call that perfect third of our Peninsula, Pebble

Beach, and what a treasure it is. Very often taken for granted, praised or maligned for too many or not enough golf courses, trees, homes, resorts, it is as close as we can get to a Crown Jewel. Current management seems to recognize the sacred trust passed to them. It was a close call when that big guy from Denver was in charge! Pebble is a major employer as well as a magnet for the rich and famous who spend big bucks on nice homes and spread money well outside the gates. Speaking of gates, back in the good old days I think it cost 50 cents admission. This was serious since four bits was a pretty good piece of change. Oh hi, we'd say. Going to see the Fosters, or the Jones, or the Jacksons. Sooner or later, minor embarrassment as the gatekeeper called our "destinations" to verify. Easy now, on Sundays, to avoid the $9.25 by going to church! No cheating! OK. Round it out and put Ten in the plate.... Back then, entrance to The Drive was important. Sure, we could park with our honey at The Point, but for real seclusion nothing like a back road in the pines.

I think you too have noticed the wonderful polite and helpful staff all over Pebble, from Heidi with the Smokey The Bear hat at the Carmel gate, Joey in The Beach club, to the valets, gardeners, security, waiters, and of course, the annual visit of the goats. OK, the deer, too.

● ● ● ● ●

Among My Souvenirs

On these rainy afternoons, take a little time to dig into an old desk drawer, that cardboard box up on the closet shelf, or the antique sea chest under Grandma's embroidered cushions. If you're like me, it'll take you back fifty years or more, and some of the stuff will go back fifty years before then. Oh, I know, we can pull up anything we want on the Internet, and that's fun, too, on a rainy day, but look! Here's my first stamp collection! What a thrill it was to get those fat envelopes in the mail, "on approval," and Valuable Stamps, Free! Lots of the King of England, and the handsome Prince of Romania. And best of all, the Princess of Alba, the Goya nude, and there she was, breasts and all! And here's dozens of envelopes, First Day Covers, and hundreds of stamps that need to be sorted. I'll bet these are <u>valuable!</u>

_____Dig a little deeper in the box, and there are those Love Letters! From the summer love, almost forgotten. Gosh, did she keep those from you, too? (Isn't it just wonderful to have FaceBook and YouTube, and Blackberry! Makes your heart flutter)

And a dance card, not filled out. A whole pile of Valentines, and good grief, some report cards! And believe it or not, "Philbrick is a very fine student!" Very early comment.

Our grandparents and great aunts spent hours on scrapbooks, pasting pictures, clippings, and old photos, recipes, and greeting cards and since they were meant for us, years and years away, take the time to see what they thought important way back then. General Douglas MacArthur got plenty of coverage, and before, him Lindberg, and then the kidnapping. And Boulder Dam, and Bixby Bridge, The Golden Gate, and Treasure Island!

And by golly, a copy of Mechanix llustrated, 1949! Now <u>that</u> is a real archeological treasure! The ads alone, on the late fringe of the good old days, give great direction and hope for the years to come. Charles

Atlas, with Dynamic Tension! ART for Pleasure and Profit! LEARN RADIO by Practicing in Spare Time! Don't Miss the Chance of a Lifetime... TELEVISION! Start Your Own Business... Metalize Baby Shoes! <u>Inventors Wanted!</u> LEARN MEAT CUTTING, Easily, Quickly, Study At Home! Gosh, think of what "might have been!"

And the articles! "World's Fastest Woman Driver." Her car was named "Drool." How to build boats, planes, models, and step stools. And Grow Apples as Big as Your Head! On the back cover, "Prove CAMEL Mildness In <u>Your</u> T Zone!"

Well, more opportunities missed. But back to hobbies. Here's the start of the coin collection. Didn't last long. A fine assortment of Cigar bands, and even the Lionel Train Catalog. An envelope of the dry cement to mix in construction of the Strombecker wooden airplane models. (Later plastic kits just didn't have the right thrill.) Ought to take the stack of Kodak negatives, have them printed, see who's there. Maybe next week.

Just put all this stuff back in the box, put a note on top, "Don't Throw Out." You never can tell.

* * * * *

Out Of The Mud

"Out of the mud grows the lotus." So said good old Don Sherwood, and I find it comforting to remember in these semi difficult times. For instance, I heard or read that some icons of the good old days are bubbling back up. Yep! Avon Calling! Mary Kay, Fuller Brush! Direct sales, they happily tout, is a recession proof business! And don't be surprised if your neighbor invites you to a Tupperware or Lingerie party! Sure, all these opportunities and diversions survive, and even prosper in some parts of the country, but it has been awhile since they knocked on my door, or yours, for that matter.

Mom always swore to never buy another thing at the door, but she sure did like that Fuller vegetable brush, free, of course, and two dollars later things she treasured until that nice guy knocked again. I don't think a Christmas went by without Avon soap under the tree. Best of all, the soap imbedded with rope to hang around your neck. Hard to suds up beneath the belly button, but the concept was good.

While I suppose the local merchants might object, I wouldn't be surprised if the milkman arrived again at our doorstep. Forget the homogenized, bring back those great bottles with the cream at the top. And let the cat lick the lid!

With good Farmer's Markets hither and yon, we really don't need to have vegetables delivered to our door, but what fun it was to stroll out to the curb, pick out a head of lettuce and a pound of peaches. I know, most of our markets, super or otherwise, are happy to deliver your order, some of it already cooked and ready to eat. All you have to do is set the table!

Memory weakens, but I think I remember an old Ford truck with fish for sale, and then the super summer sound of the Ice Cream Man! For sure, there was the Milk Nickel bar, vanilla ice cream on a stick, dipped in chocolate, and every once in awhile, a Free Stick! Next time around the Ice Cream Man exchanged the stick, licked very clean, for another Milk Nickel!

I do recall some difficulties in direct sales, me with the Liberty Magazine bag, and later, Christmas cards, salve, and postage stamps. But the thrill of it all, I still recall. "No thanks, Sonny, but how about some lemonade and cookies!" And speaking of lemonade, be generous this summer when the kids down the block set up their stand. I could be wrong, but I think maybe Warren Buffett started out that way. Or was it Bill Gates? No, no! It was Leon Panetta!

*   *   *   *   *

Turn The Radio On!

Just when I was a little short on memories, up popped Dave Sailer prompting me on the glorious days of Radio!, flashing back to the 1930s and 1940s! Be careful what you read. Almost all these great shows can be found on the Internet if you fish around, and before you know it, there's another afternoon wrapped up in nostalgia. Even comparing these drama to current TV excess, most of them stand up very well. Good writing, timing, talent and story lines that pull you back. Just to riffle through a few, how about Captain Midnight!, Little Orphan Annie, and from Ovaltine a decoder badge!. Jack Armstrong, The All American Boy! (Have you *tried* Wheaties!), The Green Hornet!, Flash Gordon, Inner Sanctum, and The Shadow..."Who knows what evil lurks in the heart of man?," and on and on. And not quite so famous, but a thrill just the same, "General Shafter Parker And His Circus" with a villain called Mouse. They all got us through the Depression and WW2, always reminding us of The American Way.

My favorite was "I Love a Mystery, with Jack, Doc, and Reggie. " Plenty of blood and mayhem, with cliff hanging chills and thrills. One series featured an "Old Mansion," and a mysterious organ played Brahms Lullaby just as murder was about to strike! Written by Carlton E Morse, whose even more famous and enduring stories, "One Man's Family." A serial drama, it played over twenty-seven years, 3,256 performances. Try the Internet on that one, hear organist Paul Carson start the show, and you're right back at Sea Cliff in San Francisco with Father Barbour and Mother Fanny, with their kids, Hazel, Claudia, Clifford and Jack. With a few cast changes along the way it was also a TV series from 1949 to 1952, continuing on radio until 1959. The TV cast included such future stars as Eva Marie Saint, Tony Randall, and Mercedes McCambridge. Like so many radio shows, it was easier to imagine faces to the voices, than to actually see them on TV. The NBC studio broadcasting from San

Francisco was at 111 Sutter, famous for other reasons, but more about that some other time. Well, we got to know the Barbour family just as well as the neighbors next door. They were *real*. And just as real, of course, were Ma Perkins, and Vic and Sade. Now don't fret. I'll get on to Fibber McGee, Jack Benny, and a few others, sooner or later, but right now look back to Doctor

I.Q. "I have a lady in the balcony, Doctor"... and two silver dollars and a box of Mars Bars if she can answer this question!"

And then, setting an early stage for talent shows, was Major Bowes Amateur Hour!

He was notably tough on the talent with a big Gong! when he disapproved.

I drift now into "funny books," which deserve several columns, but to wind this up, I remember Billy Batson, who became Captain Marvel when he said the magic word, Shazam! We never said the word quite right, but that's OK! Look how well we turned out!

Reading and observing the current rash of vandalism I had considered doing a story on the harmless old pranks we pulled back in the good old days. "Upon further review" I have decided otherwise. I have just wasted an hour looking at all the "Prank" sites on the Internet and don't want to encourage any action that would result in eternal regret. (Some fun to read, but not to act on.)

As I look back I guess pranks were to flaunt authority, get away with something, or pick on somebody for any number of reasons. Somebody other than your parents. Most of these pseudo sins were silly, sometimes stupid or dangerous, or even destructive. OK, sometimes funny, but not usually. For goodness sake, why did we steal signs? But there they were, trophies! STOP... GO... NO FISHING... CIGARS 5 CENTS... SOFT SHOULDER!... KEEP OFF THE GRASS!

A friend of mine, now well along in years, recalls driving through town with friends knocking over potted plants, then for an encore, tossing lawn furniture in the hotel pool. Caught, of course, and paid a heavy price, the thrill of "getting away with it" was brief and fleeting.

Sooner or later those delinquents in an East Bay community who take delight in smashing mailboxes will be caught and sent to prison. That really is a Federal Offense, and the senior citizens so violated will make sure their names are published.

In a generation slightly before mine out houses were a favorite target, one, in fact, left on the steps of PG High. Quarters glued to the sidewalk, purses or wallets pulled on a string from the grasp of the curious, soap in the city fountain, and of course, Joy Buzzers, Whoopee cushions, and exploding cigarettes. We've come a long way!

Phone ID has taken away concern re poor old Prince Albert in the can, and with The Weather Channel no need ask "Is the coast clear?"

Teachers were always in danger. In Mrs. Mello's class we all pushed our books on the floor at the same second, a satisfying rumble, and then embarrassment, shame, and regret.

In college pranks soared to new heights, many inspired by tales of Doodles Weaver at Stanford. I dare not repeat some of the most creative for fear of plagiarism, but the Sigma Chi Trophy Caper is too good not to be shared. This at University of New Mexico, circa 1950, the Phi Delts (since removed from campus) entered the Sigma Chi house while they were away singing to their Sweetheart, and made off with the trophy collection, deposited one on each of the university golf course greens, and then alerted fraternity row. Lovely pandemonium across the fairways, crime never solved. One collateral damage… a sweet little Tri Delt from Santa Fe lost her underpants in one of the sand traps, reason never fully disclosed. Luckily her Mom had sewn her name in all her stuff, the item discovered, then posted in the Student Union for recovery.

Crazy kids!

. . . . .

Over Easy!

Recalling sounds of the good old days in Pacific Grove, our hometown, something I don't think you'll hear any more are chickens. Somewhere along the line I suppose the city passed a law against them, and while not every home had a hen house, most people had fresh eggs. There was a nice sort of cluck, cluck from back yards, and a strident cock a doodle doo from a rooster or two. Some folks were bothered, I guess, but nobody complained about the sea gulls, and come to think of it, they seem a little scarcer now, too!

Brother Tom had an old pet red hen named "Broken Toe," for obvious reasons, and she delivered nice brown eggs every other day. Followed Tom around the yard like a puppy and produced a modest amount of manure while she was at it. There were a lot of rabbit hutches around town, just for pets, of course, and now and then there was a loose rabbit hopping between houses.

Plenty of Easter ducks, but by the end of summer they fit in happily at El Estero. My mom had a parrot named Pancho that now lives with brother Tom and six other parrots in his office in Jackson. Old. Been known to lay an egg. Parrots do that.

Slightly more up scale were the pigeons and Dick de Lorimier was King of the Cote, with dozen of homers, tumblers, and fantails. Once upon a time I signed up for a taxidermy class, one pigeon required. I think Mr. Ruth was the instructor and demonstrated the humane way to put the bird to be stuffed to sleep. I'll show you some time. So off to de Lorimier's I went and bought a nice bird for a dollar, not explaining to Dick the planned demise. Since the next class was couple of weeks away I installed my pigeon in a nice coop above the back porch, with plenty of food and a nice view. Believe it or not, you can get attached to a pigeon. Time for the class, and I just couldn't do it! I opened the coop and out he went, a straight line back to de Lorimier's out on Lighthouse. I didn't have the nerve to ask for my dollar back.

And speaking of pigeons, you will remember the early days of television when most of the houses in town had spindly aluminum antennas wired to the chimneys. Well, in flew a wave of wild pigeons, big and black, and they roosted on those antennas just long enough to bend or break them, and away they went. All over town, antennas either gone or pointing down!

Not much notable livestock in town, although I do remember Ray Lugo riding a white horse up Fountain Avenue to Pine. Best of all, the Donkey Baseball at the softball field.

I think there are more deer and raccoons now than then, and not in the same category, a lot fewer salmon and abalone. Still plenty of butterflies!

* * * * *

A Spoonful of Sugar

Remember that old saying, "Everybody talks about the weather, but nobody does anything about it." Well, by Gore, I guess we are trying to do something about it, but the same thing can be said about Health Care. Everybody talks about it, but nothing seems to get done. OK, that's not fair. Just look back on the good old days and admit that medicine has come a long, long way. Now I realize I'm lucky, being seriously mature and in reasonably good shape, and aside from a decent gene pool, I give all the credit to Health Care! When I was a kid I think one doctor did it all, or most of it, but of it wasn't for my current team, I would be dead and buried, or a least blind and ugly.....or uglier! Doctors White, Whisler, and Eric Del Piero save my eye sight, Dr. Richard Hambley does the best he can with face and skin cancers, and Dr. Wally Holz takes care of the rest of me with a little outside help now and then. Why just last week he assured me that my heart would last me the rest of my life! Doctors Love and Pierre do my teeth, and you should see me smile! Include Drs. Ravalin and Luba and you can see why I'm an expert on Health Care! And friends, none of these gentlemen are over paid! Sure, it costs a little more, and I don't remember health insurance in the 1930s and 1940s, but it seems to me that what goes into doctor and hospital bills sooner or later filters back into the economy. Money at work means people at work. CHOMP hires a lot of people and let's face it. You wouldn't want to be treated by the cheapest Doc in town!

I haven't broken a bone recently and I understand from my MD brother that new lightweight fiber glass and plastic casts have taken the place of the old plaster of Paris creations. Now that's worth spending a few more bucks.

But what fun in the old days to write messages of love and encouragement on those heavy casts! Those few obscene messages were wiped out with white shoe polish.

I hope I never experience water boarding, but I don't think it could be much worse than mustard plasters. First sign of chest distress and Mom would slap on one of those and tell me to lie still! Must have worked. I'm still here.

Almost trite to remember cod liver oil, but just mix that with a little Brewer's Yeast, and you wouldn't dare get sick. Still no cure for the common cold, but back in the good old days at University of New Mexico the infirmary happily injected us with some sort of serum, but I think most good came from the high altitude and Coors in a keg.

For serious colds, we were issued a bottle of Elixer of Terpin Hydrate, laced, I think, with a little codeine. Very effective before an eight o'clock class. I'll have to look it up. In the meantime, UNM Medical School is now one of the top ten in the country.

I'll you this, friends. I never met a doctor I didn't like! Well, some were better than others, but after all. Best doc story – really true – Doctor Spencer Hoyt, the one that pulled off my damaged big toe nail, among other things, once upon a time in the 1920s, was a medical missionary in Korea.

Took out his own appendix! Try that on virtual TV.

* * * * *

Resolve!!!

7:00 a.m.   Up and at 'em! Feeling great! Brush teeth, shave, step on the scale, and admit to myself that it would be a good idea to cut out the wine for a few days, drop four or five pounds, and clear the head, etc.

8:00 a.m.   Feeling even better. Coffee, walk on the beach, and think maybe cut back on the wine, not cut out. Maybe one glass, easing back on the calories, so to speak.

12:00 noon   Feeling better than ever, and looking forward to that one glass of wine at 5:00. Actually, probably makes sense to have two glasses, just to modify the schedule.

3:00 p.m.   After nap, remember that Jesus said "Wine is good for the stomach." Actually, it was "A little wine is good for the stomach" and medical science has confirmed that it is also good for the heart.

4:00 p.m.   Life can be difficult, and who's to say what deprivation we need to endure. There will probably be a better time to cut back on the vino, this not being a good time to bring on emotional distress. Nevertheless, two good glasses ought to calm the nerves. Maybe cut back on the cheese.

5:00 p.m.   Feeling better than ever, and if two glasses can be this effective, maybe a third, just tonight. At least, just one bottle, 750ml, therefore ensuring a good night's sleep.

"Sleep, that knits the raveled edge of care… !

*   *   *   *   *

Roughing It!

Flashing back to the 1940s, Jerry Fry and I shouldered into our 90-pound packs and climbed over Kearsarge Pass into the High Country. Young, strong, in perfect shape, into the wilderness for a couple of weeks roughing it. Plenty of food, fishing gear, maps, matches, and extra socks. Most of the 90 pounds per was food. We had both honed our outdoor skills in the Big Sur country, struggling up the Pine Ridge Trail to Ventana, Barlow, and beyond. Pitched a great camp by a beautiful lake, had fresh trout for supper.

Boughs of fresh cedar, as recommended in the old Boy Scout Manual, made up soft beds under our pup tent. Not as soft as advertised, but tired as we were, soft enough.

Although we hung our food high out of the reach of bears or chipmunks, it wasn't high enough and that first night a bear or two cleaned us out. All that was left was a can of dried carrots. Not to worry, plenty of trout... except that was the day they stopped biting. The mosquitoes hadn't.

A passing pack train shared some biscuits, but after a couple of glorious days, we hiked back over Kearsarge, down to Onion Meadows, and hitchhiked out to food and family. Still, as you can tell, sixty some odd years later, a memorable trip.

Now, flashforward to roughing it in style, comfort, and class. Good thing since the years have taken a toll. My son, Scott and grandson Greg hiked with me a mile through a beautiful meadow and forest, at 8200 feet, to the Sequoia High Sierra Camp, me with maybe 15 pounds of underwear, socks, and a razor. The hike in really sets the stage, but if you are old, infirm, tired or lazy, they will jeep you up the back road. The camp is delightful, deluxe, and perfect. Tent cabins with sheets and Serta Perfect Sleep mattresses are better, believe it or not, than cedar boughs and a pup tent. With spectacular views and high altitude air, the camp is the pet project built three years ago by yep! Tennessee couple, Burr and Suzanne Hughes. As you would expect, a mix of Southern and Sierra hospitality and a charming staff. Hike to your heart's content, and hot showers! And, oh, yeah. The food. It has been a long time since I ate at Ahwahnee, and as we said in the old days, "This is better than Ernie's!" A worldclass chef, with tables set, and desserts you will dream over. And no dried carrots!

I bring all this up, since some things are really better than the good old days.

And the cost? Well, it does cost a few cents more to go first class, and as we said in the shoe business, Quality is remembered long after price has been forgotten! ...and it helps to have a generous son!

* * * * *

Yearbook Archives

Here we are again, Yearbook season, and what a tug, not only to look at those new ones of your grandkids, but to riffle through and flashback to those of ours, signed by classmates fifty years ago. (How about sixty?) The college editions almost too big to handle, but those from our local high schools, just right. When I find myself running short of memories, I flip open The Sea Urchin, PG High's annual time capsule.

More smiles than tears, and we realize that those years were our *lives!* We look now at our teen aged grandkids, wonder at their tensions, traumas and troubles, then solid, loving, and filled with hope, and not knowing it. Were we the same? Look at those bright eyes in the senior pictures, see the wonderful silliness of the junior girls, and timid, scared faces of the freshmen and sophomores! Under the senior pictures are the activities we thought important. Basketball 2,3, 4. Senior Play, Typing award, Scholarship Society, 2, 3, 4. Mother's Tea, 3. Track 2, 3, 4. Garland Girl 1, 2, 3. Go ahead. Fill in your own blanks! We had a lot of transfers, both in and out. Remember the world in 1947 and still a big military presence here in our hometown.

It would break my heart, and maybe yours, to list those bright faces that blossomed, bloomed, then passed away. I see that the girl kissed as a sophomore died last month. But look, look! That beautiful gal with the lovely voice, is still with us! So she lives in Red Bluff! Or is it Redding? So what! And our Olympic pole vaulter, happy and humming, in Oregon! Our Queen of the May, still dancing in Seattle! And good grief, look at our chiefs, doctors, lawyers, plumbers, carpenters, craftsmen, moms, and dads. Look at how well we turned out.

I flash back to 1945, Monterey Hi track meet and I was running my first race. Light weight, 3:30, running fast and scared. With 50 yards to go, ahead of the pack, and Joe
Canaya shouts at me, "Keep your head down!" I did, and I won. Joe was

a senior at the time. Coach Baskin said he was the most talented and promising athlete he had ever seen... if he'd just quick smoking! In 1946 Joe was driving home and between Fort Ord and Seaside, a crash. At the hospital he waited while they took care of his passengers, and he died before they got to him. He still has that shy grin in the 1945 Sea Urchin, and a list of the things he thought important. You can look it up. And thanks, Joe, for the good advice. I didn't always take it.

Look at your yearbook and review the notes and autographs, everything from the heartfelt to the slightly obscene. "What," said my mother. "What did he mean by *that!*"

Lots of "Best wishes," and "Swell." "Good luck," and in some cases, cryptic reference to an experience long forgotten. My Latin teacher wrote "Pax Vobiscum," I'll have to look it up. Here and there, a tear or two, and a still red print of lovely lips. And the note from that awesome junior girl... "OK," she wrote. "One of these days!"

Well, that day hasn't shown up... yet! But there she smiles, in the Sea Urchin!

●　●　●　●　●

Confessions of a Shoe Dog

Best job I ever had, except of course, for the last one, was selling shoes at Hinkel's in Albuquerque. Then there were the years as a bellhop, but that's another story.

Hinkel's was about as high style as you could get in New Mexico in the early 1950s and this required a coat and tie, no less.

Winding up my elongated college career with only a couple of years to go I needed to eat and a fraternity brother figured I had enough inherent con and class to sell shoes with him, and there I was! Learning the shoe business turned out to be a pretty good background for the investment business, but more about that later.

In that day and age the term "shoe dog" was a badge of honor, a respected profession indeed. I have noticed recently some disdain when I have used that title with people selling shoes, but they doubtless have little knowledge of the rich tradition and heritage that we old shoe dogs enjoyed. Ah well, part of the general decline of things.

The standard line was that everybody is born barefoot and everybody needed what we had to sell. And then too, this was a business you could work up in, an intriguing thought indeed, but highly overrated. I mean, not that there wasn't a certain amount of entertainment, so to speak, but the real challenge was getting the right fit. I should rephrase that, but I don't want to lose my train of thought.

This was all before Imelda Marcos, but there were shoe junkies a plenty, and Larry and Earle who owned the franchise really knew how to buy what would sell in Albuquerque. High style this and that, Andrew Geller, Peacock, Town and Country, and for the casual crowd, Old Maine Trotters. Ladies and kids only, men's shoes by special order. Spike heels, platforms, ankle straps, and for the more conservative and wealthy ladies, lizard and alligator pumps. The college gals loved the Squaw Boots, horse hide soles with soft suede tops, and silver buttons, with button holes cut to fit by good old shoe dogs. By special order, high heeled tennis shoes, open toe hip boots, and bowling shoes with sandpaper soles. Not to forget Sample Shoes, usually hand made, high style, used at shoe shows to display new lines and fashion. Available for special customers at roughly a third of regular price. Primary requirement was to be able to fit into a 4B. It also helped if they were attractive, like cute.

On the serious side, how to make the presentation. A little verbal prelude before opening the box, then carefully upwrapping the tissue, then presenting the <u>right</u> shoe, held back just a little, with an added comment on it's beauty, class, and scarcity, etc, before slipping it on the extended right foot. Sometimes a little foreplay, so to speak, like a gentle massage of the metatarsal arch, helped close the sale. Now your own experience will tell you that some shoes look better <u>on</u>, looking down, than held in the hand, and that, of course, is a judgment made by the professional. Anticipation and satisfaction tend to go together, but occasionally an impatient customer would say something like "Cut the bullshit and give me the f – king shoe!" There are some people like that.

Well, on to the perfect fit. The best in the business was McPhate who had been selling shoes since the old high button days and looked like somebody's great uncle, right out of Central Casting. Honest, convincing and knew more about feet than Dr. Scholls, who he claimed to have known personally.

Needless to say there is no trick in slipping a 7½ B onto a 7½ foot. But what to do if you have a 7½ B foot and say, the closest you can come is an 8 C? Well, not to worry. First, Mac would install a couple of insoles, known as "cookies," then a little heel insert which was a pretty good idea anyway. All this, naturally in the back room, while "looking for stock." Then, as a true artist, Mac gently scraped off the 8C with his pen knife, and remarked the shoe – and the box – as 7 ½ B! Well, shoe fit like a glove, so to speak, and everybody happy! The boss claimed that Mac had crippled more people than polio, but boy could he sell shoes!

Not quite so easy with a shoe too narrow, but in the hands of good old McPhate, the shoe stretcher was very effective in going just a little wider, sometimes just the toes, sometime the whole shoe. Very dangerous with alligator and lizard which tended to split, and a split alligator was very tough to sell, no matter how good it felt.

Always in stock were some items that hadn't moved for one reason or another. Probably too ugly, or whatever, and they were marked, in code, as PMs. And boy, if you could sell a couple of PMs, your day was made. Two or three bucks extra, and that would buy a lot of tortillas, with a Kraft Dinner on the side! And then there were the shiny clips to dress up a nice pair of comfortable pumps. A couple bucks, lady, and you have another pair of shoes! And the shoe dog, of course, could buy some extra beans and rice.

The shoe career was not without some minor downsides, and this was especially true in Albuquerque on a hot, hot summer day. You may have noticed, in your own experience, that hot, sweaty feet sometimes smell bad. No other way to put it, and some unfortunates have feet that really smell bad. They usually wanted to try on shoes right after we had had lunch. BUT, the boss, ever resourceful, kept a large bottle of smelling salts just inside the stock room. Also helpful if a customer ever fainted.... I might also suggest that if you go shoe shopping without hose, take your own Peds or socks, or just let the shoe dog sell you a pair. Those loose ones in the barrel....well, you understand.

Summing up, right shoes look better than left shoes. Fit and feel are more important than style. And yes indeed, size does matter. A nice foot and a nice calf usually go together. And as always, if the shoe fits, buy it!

• • • • •

Everybody's Born Barefoot

I admit, or confess, that I do watch Oprah – sometimes – when I'm working around the kitchen, but not those dreadful stories about "makeovers" or messed up people. Just about to push the off button a couple of weeks ago, when I had a genuine flash back! Here was a shoe – I mean show – on Ladies Shoes! Now in case you wonder, I don't have a foot fetish, but more about that later. Back in the good old days, last two years of college, I sold ladies shoes at Hinkels in Albuquerque, just about as high style as you could get. I was a "shoe dog," and very proud of it! Sixty years later I see that people are still wearing shoes. Once you learn the shoe business you develop a serious study of foot wear. After all, everybody is born barefoot.

Remember, as kids, our school shoes had sharkskin toes along with a free shark tooth! Later, the Boy Scout brand got us into high school, and then we advanced to penny loafers and Spalding saddles, with the reddish soles. There were some high top Keds, and the gals wore Baby Dolls and Mary Janes with the rounded toe... sometimes. And if you were really special, and of course we all were, we got Buster Brown with his pal Tige! But back to Albuquerque.

We specialized in Andrew Geller, Peacock, Town & Country and Old Maine Trotters. If you were around the Southwest back in the good old days, you may remember Squaw Boots, very popular with the college crowd. White horsehide soles, with over the ankle suede, usually turquoise. We custom cut holes for silver buckles. Selling shoes was an art and a science, with more than a little psychology, drama and showmanship. A shoe is designed to be seen, as well as felt, on the foot. Granted, some show better in the right hand of the shoe dog, having carefully been unwrapped from the tissue. The *right* shoe shows better than the left. I notice in some salons – OK, shoe stores – the customers are left to rummage around a table, find something they might like, find a clerk, ask for a size, etc. The clerks are working on four customers at once, boxes scattered, sizes mixed. So it works, but better then, and I'll bet now, to ask the customer to please be seated, do a little analysis, check the size, find a new pair of Peds – free – a light massage of the metatarsal, and then "By golly, do I have shoe for you!"

Some shoes are really works of art, created to be worn on beautiful feet. A shoe dog appreciates a "well turned ankle," and then, the miracle of a perfect calf. This brings us to the dubious reason for spike, or stiletto heels, which do accentuate the space between ankle and knee, as well as over all height! Remember, ladies, that high heels can't be worn in Carmel without a permit. I know that's tough, but like gravity, it's the law. Fear of injury on our uneven pavement, or something like that. No arrests lately.

A student of styles, I have hoped that those pointed toes on otherwise classy pumps would fade fast away. Depends on whom you ask. Heather, at Lloyds, that fine store in Carmel, claims they are still popular and in steady demand. Across the street at Hedi's I'm told they just don't sell any more!

I have been known to compliment a ladies shoe, when warranted. Yesterday I told a nice looking lady that "I used to be in the shoe business, and that's a very nice Gucci!"

"Yeah," she said, "and I used to be a cop! Now get lost!"

Well, as they say, "If the shoe fits.... Charge it!"

* * * * *

More Library!

Since I was a little kid I've spent a lot of time in libraries, and I'll bet you have, too. My home library was in PG, on Central, down behind Holman's and across the street from the roque courts. I still wander in there now and then, and although readjusted and modernized since the 1940s, it still has that hometown feeling. I started hanging out in the kids' section, reading all the Oz books, the Twins, Bobbsey and otherwise, and then moved up to the Howard Pease sagas. Then over to the adult fiction stacks – adult fiction is different now – and read away, sometimes curled up in an overstuffed leather chair, basking in the sunlight and loving the library quiet. I notice that libraries still have that magical faint smell, of old books, a little dust and papers, and yep, even library paste.

My home library now is Harrison Memorial in Carmel, and friends, it is neat and snug, complete and perfect! In front, it's like a glorious living room, with a big fireplace, and lots of very comfortable chairs. And of course, lots of books! Kid's section down the street – Park Branch – and you can only imagine all the eager readers getting the right library start in life. If you haven't noticed, kids really like books, even better than video games, once they are exposed! It's a sacred duty of grandparents to push that reading button. Once or twice should do it!

And then, of course, there's that marvelous Monterey Library, across from the fire station. I can wander through the stacks for hours, just touching the books, and smiling at those old friends – Kenneth Roberts, Cheever, Jules Vern, Steinbeck, Ward Just, and on and on forever. Pull out a book, and find there a familiar paragraph, almost forgotten.

Just for fun, log in and up to Jimmy Buffet's "Love in the Library" and of course, Marian the Librarian, waltzing around the River City Library! Yes, I know that all librarians are beautiful. That glow comes from being around all those books! And while you're on the Internet, try You Tube – Shout It Out For Your Library!

I'm reminded of that old cliché, "If you can't read, or don't read, the results are the same." Just ask Jimmy Durante, with that minor classic, "I'll never forget the day I read a book."

OK, to wind this up, give a book for Christmas, and better yet, get your kids a library card – any library will do – and then to cap it off, send that library a few bucks with your kid's name on it!

See you in the stacks!

*　*　*　*　*

Thank You, Western Union

"Send me a kiss by wire! Honey, my heart's on fire!" And so it was in the good old days, when we sent love letters and notice of affection, by wire! Telegrams! Western Union. I realized the other day that I said I was going to send a wire. Blank look, then grandkid remembered telegrams in old movies. What a skill it was to say as much as possible in fewest possible words. Many jokes STOP, and often much confusion "What did she mean STOP? Since there was an extra charge for punctuation, STOP filled the bill, in a manner of speaking. And yes, I know the song really refers to the telephone, but that's another story.

Check your scrap book or old shoe box and you're sure to find those old telegrams, yellowed and wrinkled, messages in strips, and pasted on. Delivered to your door with news of hope, love, humor and tragedy, always quickened your heart beat when the kid on the bike pulled up to the steps. Western Union sent the last telegram in 2006 and now helps us wire money hither and yon.

You knew I had to mention the miracle and convenience of E-mail, texting, Facebook, Tweeting, and overlapping variations. All well and good, but what about Aunt Sally who doesn't know a ding dong from a Dell, or an Apple from a quince? How to wish her a Happy Birthday, or suggest you could use a modest loan? Well, there's always the telephone, and even Sally has one of those. But don't overlook the Post Office. They can use the business, and what the heck. For Christmas give Aunt Sally a laptop!

Back in the good old days I had a boss who hated to fire people, face to face. Sure enough... Western Union to the rescue...."Dear Miss Smithers, I regret to inform you...."

Miss Smithers responded with a kiss by wire, notably without affection.

There were lots of telegram specials, the most famous was the

"Singing Telegram" where the guy or gal at the door would belt out Happy Birthday or something equally appropriate.

My wife and I in the Venetian Room at the Fairmont, crowded, noisy, waiting for the Mills Brothers, and up to the table in a tux – Western Union – from your kids! he says, and the room hushes as he sings Happy Anniversary! Only slightly embarrassing...

There are a couple of telegram jokes on the Internet that are very funny, but more than slightly inappropriate for The Herald, but you can look them up. We used to tell the story about the bellhop delivering a telegram to a hotel room, hoping for a tip.

The guest... cheap... said, "Just slide it under the door!" "Can't" says the bellhop. "Why not?" says the guest. Bellhop says "It's on a plate!"

And then, the German Shephard walks in to a Western Union office, fills out the form, "Woof, Woof, Woof, Woof, Woof, Woof..." gives it to the clerk, who says, "You can add another Woof at no extra charge." German Shepherd replies, "That wouldn't make any sense at all!" Some columns are like that.

•   •   •   •   •

Gold!

The great story of the 1948 Monterey Gold rush pops up now and then, and it's about time to dust it off again. As the saying goes, gold is where you find it, and this was on the Martin property being bull dozed for the new Monterey High Music room. Seems that John Martin didn't trust banks – sound familiar?… and buried jars of gold coins all around his property. Told his kids that sooner or later he'd show them where, but by the time he was ready to tell them, he'd forgotten! Well, the dozer cracked a jar and coins were hither and yon, and there was a two or three day scramble with both good and bad guys gone nuts. If you want the real story, coin by coin, talk to Mike Maiorana. Mike about twelve at the time and just barely escaped bodily injury saving his broken jar. After some police protection and maybe a good guy or two, he got home with a decent handful of treasure. Lots more to the story, but Mike's the man. And he is a treasure himself, with Monterey history! And by the way, he still has those coins, safe in a bank, and not buried in his back yard.

Aside from the Martin property there are dozens of treasure stories, and some might even be true. The Jose Maria Sanchez stash might still be kicking around – you could look it up – but before you start tearing up parking lots or your neighbors' roses, understand that real estate today is worth more than what's buried beneath! I'm reminded by my brother, Mike, that Alvarado Street was painted gold for the centennial celebration. OK. Maybe not real gold, but the right color, anyway.

You may remember that Robert Louis Stevenson was told by an old Chinese merchant that the Indians had saved altar pieces from the Mission, hidden from "the soldiers" in a blow hole at Point Lobos. RLS couldn't find the blowhole, and neither could I. At least he wrote a book!

Other treasure abounds. Years ago somebody found a diamond – yep, a real diamond – in the Big Sur River, up above Ventana. Greyish in color, poor quality, but a diamond still. Let's not even touch the jade story, or abalone pearl. I did read once about ambergris – whale vomit – and heard it was insanely valuable, sought after for perfume manufacture. And by golly, one day I found a big glop of something strange on Asilomar Beach. Took it home. Dad shook his head, said take it to Hopkins tomorrow and find out.

It was gone the next morning, doubtless taken by an astute raccoon.

My Dad was not immune to treasure fever and he came upon a very authentic map with the location of Joaquin Murrieta's loot. Seems Joaquin was headed south just ahead of the posse, saddlebags loaded with gold. Just East of what is now Puente he buried the bags under a small Sycamore tree, marked the spot, and rode away. Dad wasn't sure of what happened to Joaquin, but he had the map, and that was good enough! Well, long story short, armed with a transit and a shovel, he found the exact spot! It was now a million ton concrete over pass!

I do remember something about not laying up treasure on earth, but look North to Heaven. That's close enough!

* * * * *

Car Sick!

The only thing wrong with Kernville in the 1930s was the road to and from Bakersfield. Spectacular and one of the most beautiful drives in California, it was difficult to appreciate when you were car sick to death. My Dad was the Kern County Fire Department Ranger in Kernville and we lived in a wonderful adobe house on the North end of town, right next to the river. The "ditch" was on the other side of the house with a big lawn, fishponds and cottonwood trees in between. Absolute Paradise for a kid! This was long before they plugged up the Mighty Kern and made a mighty lake, but more about that later.

A trip to Bakersfield really was a big deal, visiting relatives and stocking up on groceries not available at Brown's general store. But oh my. About five minutes into the canyon – in either direction – Dad would stop by the side of the road and let us be sick, sick, sick. My Mom was usually the first, brother Brooks, about 5 years old, was next, and me, at eight or so, followed fast. Dad, sympathetic and stoic, held my Mom's head while we groaned, retched, and hoped to die. Then he wiped our chins, lit a Camel, and away we went. Hoping to avoid accidents inside our green Chevy, he gave each of us an empty coffee can, and to this very day, a sniff of the inside of an empty coffee can takes me farther back than I really want to go.

You may remember with me the lunch counter at Owl Drug in Bakersfield. That's where I discovered BLTs, and then, Banana Splits, usually split with my Mom. I'll just skip what that has to do with the carsick story, but I think you get the picture.

Now why is this important enough to write about? Well, if you ever rode up to Kernville in the back seat, grasping a coffee can, way back then, you can really appreciate suffering and survival, just a few rocks away from the Mighty Kern.

Tilt!

I am possibly the only person you know that has never played a video game. Well, maybe Pong a long time ago, and then there was that bout with Tetris, but those date back with Canasta. My grandkids wonder what we did for fun back in the good old days and how did we fill those idle hours when we weren't delivering papers or fiddling with stamp albums.

Sad to say, but they will never really appreciate or understand our fine addiction to pinball machines. I watch the kids today fiddle their fingers with little black boxes and wonder if they would be attracted to real pinball if they were reintroduced. Would their souls tingle with the Ka Ching, Ka Ching and thrill flipping the ellusive steel balls back to the top for another run through the flashing lights! Or would prefer that insane roar that comes from the arcade room at Century Theatre.

Well, in the good old days, in good old Pacific Grove, we had pinball machines that sharpened our senses, improved our hand/eye, and kept us off the streets. I think it was a nickel a game, which computes to a penny a ball, but even with that modest cost there was smug satisfaction running up free games. If you didn't play pinball, you might not remember Lola, Lola with the long black hair. There wasn't a pinball in the county that Lola couldn't beat, and was rumored to make decent spending money taking bets. She had a fine touch with the plunger and could place the balls within a quarter inch of the bumpers and very rarely caused a Tilt! Standing behind her we noticed a certain pelvic twist or thrust that doubtless thwarted any errant roll of the ball. I understood she could shoot pretty good pool too. Yep, we had a real pool hall in Pacific Grove, up on Forest below Laurel.

Tiring of pinball we wandered over to Grand a block away and for a length of time now forgotten we skated in our own, real rink. Now we all admire those lovely ice skaters we see on TV, but there was, and is, something different and gloriously exciting watching those gals on roller skates speed, twirl, and dance across the floor. They are somehow more real, and as they come to a sudden stop at the railing and give you a smile, and take you by the hand and guide you wobbling onto the floor....! Oh Boy!

Hey, we still have Del Monte Gardens.

Well, the PG Roller Rink didn't last, and gave way to a Bowling Alley!

Yep, right there in Pacific Grove. When we needed more pinball money we set pins, I think for a dime a line. Believe me, it wasn't worth it. Easier to deliver papers. Bowling Alley gone, too, with safe and sane office space taking up the slack.

No, no video games, but still plenty to do in PG. Watch the Civil War vets play roque, something like croquet, across from the museum, and that too was a fine place to wander and wonder and spend some time. And the library! We read books! Then a stroll through Holman's or down to the beach to check the tide, then home to supper.

* * * * *

To Look Sharp!

I suspect it was the absence of nylons during World War 2 that focused special attention on legs. Girls' legs. Some of us was were born to be "leg men" with an appreciation in that direction, but still admiring the "sweater girl" look. You know what I mean.

Girls understood their God given gifts, but for some reason had to gild the lily! They actually felt compelled to shave their legs! I guess they still do, but this was not an easy thing in the good old days. Razor blades today are marvels of technology, but back in the forties they were imperfect and dangerous. I think every leg I saw was scraped and scarred, especially across the shin. Girls showed up at school with patches of toilet paper covering that morning's wound, but the rest of the leg was smooth as a baby's bottom.

Having just learned to scrape the fuzz off our faces with Gillette Blues, we nicked every inch from our Adams apple to our cheek bones, hoping that those patches of toilet paper would keep us from bleeding to death! Sometimes a styptic pencil – alum – applied to the open wound staunched the flow, but boy, did it burn. Also a very neat trick to shave around the acne!

Well, the gang at Gillette knew a market when they saw one. Even shaved themselves1 Modern technology produced the Lady Gillette along with the Super Mach Multi Blade Shaving System, and unless we look sideway too fast instead of looking in the mirror, we can pat on the aftershave without fear or pain.

The first time Paul Varian, Pacific Grove's hometown barber, trimmed my side burns with a straight razor I had no idea what was happening. Did he not understand that all I wanted was a haircut? It was a rite of passage, and I didn't realize it at the time. And my ears were intact, and after a splash of Bay Rum I felt I had grown up, just a little.

Well, after the war, nylons came back, and then panty hose, and bare legs showed up mostly at the beach or on the tennis courts. My last two years of college I worked as a ladies shoe salesman – high styles, high heels, and high prices – and developed a very professional leg specialty. I'll be happy to discuss it some time. And of course the sweater girl style went out with the burn the bra era. Yeah, yeah. I remember. "What God has forgotten, they stuff with cotton," and I suspect even to this very day!

Back to high school, I did notice that the girl from Sacramento, a summer friend, had classic golden legs, never shaved, and enhanced with a whisper of golden down!

She later married well, and moved to South America.... but that's another story....

*　*　*　*　*

Just Before Dawn!

I was born in 1930, a depression kid, and although never depressed, I suspect that the experience might have had something to do with my attitude today. You know, like "Out of the mud grows the lotus." To tell the truth, I didn't know what a Depression was, and I don't think I heard the word until it was all over. My parents were married in May, 1929, right before the Crash, and always said it wasn't their fault!

My brothers and I grew up right through it all, thinking that was just the way things were. I don't remember any extravagances, except that Lionel train for Christmas, 1938, but we weren't hungry, thread bare, or medically deprived. Mom did walk a few extra blocks to buy soup bones and hamburger on sale, but when a hobo knocked on the back door there was always enough for a sandwich. My bike was a third hand Schwinn and – luckily – we couldn't afford the accordion, with lessons thrown in. Most of us earned our own allowances, selling Liberty Magazine, stamps, soap and greeting cards, door to door. We did get to go to the 1939 Worlds Fair on Treasure Island, but that's another story. We had some well to do relatives in Lincoln, Nebraska, and every Christmas they sent us a box of hand-me-downs. I remember a brown over coat from Marshall Field in Chicago, just right for an eight-year-old. Over the years all of us wore that coat, handed down from one kid to another. My dad thanked them, sending back Christmas greens and mistletoe!

In Bakersfield the Okie kids, barefoot and tattered overalls, would show up outside the school, for a cup of milk and an apple. They were quiet, polite, and hungry. Their parents were willing to work for next to nothing. Jobs, worse than scarce. Copies of Grapes of Wrath burned in the streets. The World War was still in memory. FDR was both hated and loved... mostly loved.

Through it all, we didn't realize the stress on our parents.

But if you were there, friends, you remember the thrill, the reassurance, and the pride when we turned up the Philco, and Kate Smith sang our solemn prayer, "God Bless America," and it wouldn't hurt for us to sing it again, right now! And then, of course, came Pearl Harbor and the Depression was officially over. Pretty heavy price, but a lot of prosperity between the next wars. And the Okie kids? Well, a couple of them showed up at Pacific Grove High School, and later on to Cal.

Now just a little comment on our current gloom and doom. First, Never Sell America Short! Like you, I've been through a lot of ups and downs. Just remember, at the top of every cycle, stock market or real estate, the experts are almost overwhelmingly optimistic. At the very bottom, lots of advice from the "nattering nabobs of negativism."

Chicken Little is right, they tell us, and worse is just around the corner!

They didn't ring a bell at the top, and they won't at the bottom, either. That's what rear view mirrors are for.

It wasn't too long ago I heard... "A million five for that house? I could have should have bought it for less than half that!" OK, Pal, Here's your chance!

*   *   *   *   *

Early Housekeeping

Back in the good old days we got married a lot younger than the current set of lads and lassies. Like 19 and 21. I'll leave alone the possible contributing factor of "permissiveness" which may or may not have sprung from the sixties. It seems that every day we hear of a couple happily announcing their intent to marry now that they have a brand new baby, or least, as we used to call it, "a bun in the oven." Wedding gowns are now constructed to accentuate the obvious, or so to say. OK. Not always, but sometimes. I will also acknowledge there seemed to be more preemies back in the good old days. (Just for the record I was a preemie myself, but "proper" by ten months.)

This came to mind recently as I pruned my book shelves and remembered the glorious days of being young marrieds in the 1950s. We set up house as best we could, counting our nickels and dimes, steak the first few days after pay day, then Kraft Dinner for the rest of the month. "Not much money, honey, but ain't we got fun!"

Furniture? Well, right after the bed, or at least the mattress, came the kitchen table. Most of us sophisticates joined the Book of The Month Club, which brings me back to these many years later, pruning the library. Everybody had a bookcase, four cement blocks, from the construction site around the corner, and two planks or ply wood. There, along with used textbooks, stood the four volumes by Winston Churchill, starting with "The Gathering Storm." Solid, thick, with red jackets! And then, possibly since a book or two was free, "no obligation," many of us signed with The Classics Club. Tan, tweedy covers, titles on the spine, touched with gold, an intellectual red. Aristotle! Plato! Omar Khayyam! Right there with Dr. Spock!

And speaking of Spock, my bride's sorority sisters, who had never been pregnant – maybe not even exposed – had plenty of advice, most of it wrong, as soon as she was "great with child." Despite the advice, he was happily born, fourteen months after the wedding, then new sets of advice from mother in law and mother. All good!

The firstborn were put on earth to lead us through the new job parenting. They suffered through mysterious rashes, colic, and second hand smoke (we really didn't know) all teaching us how to handle the next kid.

Historians, years from now, will note in our starter homes of the 1950s, not only the books, but the multi colored candle wax encrusted wine bottles! They were young family treasures, sometimes almost a foot across!

Having minored in bridge with the rest of the young marrieds; that was about the extent of our social life. The quality of bridge, however, declined with our ability to buy a little more beer.

There were three kinds of wine – red, white, and pink. Attempts to make home brew usually ended with bottles exploding in the middle of the night. And speaking of beer, we opened our Burgie with a church key. Hollow core Philippine mahogany doors with screwed on legs – or cement blocks – made great coffee tables, until in later years hatch covers were the deal. We kept our pretzels in monkey pod bowls, and those of us who had had Navy duty in Japan, brought home Noritake china. The plates were fifties stylish, but didn't do too well in the dishwasher. The guys who went to Europe came back with Cuckoo clocks.

There was also a brief fad, making beer mugs out of wine bottles. Why? Made no sense. And Kraft Cheese glasses! Maybe they'll bring them back.

I suppose we can still thaw frozen orange juice, but hard to get milk delivered to the door. Mr. Birdseye gave us frozen peas and Chef Boyardee helped us nourish our kids on Spaghetti Os. They all turned out very well, thank you! And so did we!

● ● ● ● ●

Yeah, Yeah, Yeah!

The Beatles tribute, Yeah, Yeah, Yeah at Pac Rep in Carmel will flash you back quicker than you can say Yellow Submarine, and friends, you've got two more weeks to enjoy the show. My good old days were a little before the Beatles changed the world, but they should be just right for you. A performance with the Fab Four will take you right back, make you laugh and grin as you sing along, clap your hands, wave your arms, and do a little dance in the aisle! You'll shout out "I Wanna Hold Your Hand" and Lucy is still in the sky with diamonds! On top of that, you'll watch lovely Lydia Lyons sing, shout, and shake it!

Oh, how I envied that talent on the stage. Watching the Bach Bunch it seems to me that while they certainly enjoy what they're doing, they don't have quite as much *fun* as the Beatles Bunch.

I *know* that had I *really* worked on it I could have excelled at the guitar, the drums, and the keyboard. I did pick up the tambourine in kindergarten, although a touch slow on the triangle. Most of my musical efforts have had a certain Charley Brown futility and I suspect that many of you can sympathize. How wonderful it seems when Gerry Williams sits down at the piano and riffles through Star Dust. Never took lessons!

Or Sam Wright blue grassing a banjo! Above all else, I longed to play the banjo, but fear of fingering failure killed that dream.

I took one lesson on a borrowed violin, then fell out of a tree and broke my arm. Close call. I struggled at the piano for years – just like you – and have one piece in my program, and a little shaky at that. Wow! Didn't the harmonica look like fun, and easy!

Paper route money bought a beautiful Hohner, but alas, my mouth was too big or too small. The sweet potato ocarina had some promise, but never fulfilled. It required certain finger dexterity that was foreign to me. Friends encouraged a try at a recorder, but again, just a touch beyond my talent. I did have some limited success with an auto harp, but after the basic chords, I lost interest. No magic.

There is, however, musical hope! I wandered in to Carmel Music Live at The Barnyard the other day and wandered out with a top of the line ukelele. I have mastered one chord which is all you need for Happy Birthday. Beyond that, however, comes the old finger problem. With hot compresses, Advil, and practice, I'm told I might get " Ain't She Sweet." Swell, but just look at those guys with the guitars! Watch their fingers! Good Grief!

Well, time to warm up that old Kazoo, take it to the next Beatles show. Might even start a Kazoo club, just like the Ukelele gang! Only trouble there, it's hard to sing with a Kazoo in your mouth. Thank goodness we still have the Mitch Miller records.

I don't dance too well, either, but you know how it is. Remember the good old days?

* * * * *

Paint!

It's been roughly 70 years since I gave up becoming an artist. Flash back with me to the fifth grade – maybe fourth – when it was a big deal to rinse out the paint brushes in the cloakroom sink. I suspect that now the Art hour uses marker pens, but back in the s it was watercolors and daubing the primary colors. Cleaning the brushes after school was right up there with knocking chalk dust out of the felt erasers. It was good citizenship at work, and much appreciated, or at least tolerated, by the teacher.

One fine afternoon the art teacher told our special few how to draw faces, a necessary skill if you intended to draw faces. Follow this closely. First, draw an oblong circle, roughly the shape of the intended head. Right in the middle, half way down – or up – went the eyes. Half way down from the eyes, came the mouth. Then half way between the eyes and the mouth was the bottom of the nose. The top of the nose somewhere near the eyes. We all went to work, I think with crayons – Binney and Smith – and teacher smiled and praised Doris, Sally, and Richard suggesting futures in the National Gallery. She stopped, glowered over my work, and wasn't even gentle! In a loud voice, dripping with scorn, she started in on the all wrong oblong, and that I obviously didn't know what middle or half meant, and that I would *never* be able to draw a face, and that it was lucky I didn't try to draw a horse! Now having very caring parents, I wasn't used to such abuse, but the damage was done, and I haven't drawn a face since, or even a horse. To hell with the paintbrushes! And she could by golly clean her own black board erasers!

This all flashed back the other day as I wandered through our world-class museum at La Mirada. No human could have created those images, at least not without the hand of God, or at least early encouragement in the cloakroom. Even strolling through Carmel, glancing at galleries, with everything from superb to slight, I feel just a little inadequate. But then I remember the thrill of painting by numbers! What fun to brush or dab the

27 blue into the 27 slot! Shaking just a little gave a very artistic edge, running over to 28, even better when cat walked across the canvas drying on the dining room table. For those of us who still have trouble with oblongs, but yearn to create, Aaron Brothers still stocks the paint by numbers kits. I also suggest that you check out a few Picassos and note that he not only had trouble with oblongs but Good Grief! Look at his eyes!

Well, friends, there are other means of self-expression. Try cooking, gardening, or wallpapering, and I understand that yoga calms the soul. And if all else fails, you can write!

* * * * *

Thanks a Lot!

Whether or not we think turkey is over rated, it's part of the deal and we might as well make the best of it. Most complaints concern the doneness, either over or under, and seldom just right. The white cooks faster than the dark, a serious problem since all turkeys have both. Great solution on NPR last week. Get the bird at room temp, then pack ice on the breast, getting the white colder than the dark, and presumably white and dark done perfectly at the same time. It is suggested that the ice packs be held in place with an Ace bandage, or possibly a bra, during the chilling process. Hard to explain the vision of all this if somebody walks into the kitchen. Very important to remove the Ace Bandage and the ice before actually cooking.

For some reason long forgotten. in the good old days it seemed routine to get up at five in the morning on Thanksgiving to start the turkey. Now we shove it in at a decent hour, ready for dinner in the afternoon. I guess back then we planned to sit down sometime around midday. Before we ate, though, we always delivered four or five made up plates to neighbors and grateful friends. Then the typical Norman Rockwell scene, heads bowed with thanks. Well, not quite.

As you may realize, part of the holiday tradition, whether it's Christmas, Thanksgiving, or the Fourth of July is a cup or two of cheer, earlier than usual. After all, the Pilgrims knocked down plenty of beer, maybe mead, and goodness knows about the Indians. At any rate, at our house in PG, especially when we were all adults, the atmosphere was thankful as hell, and just a touch raucous. One of us read the Wall Street Journal Thanksgiving story, Mom passed out appropriate Bible verses for each of us to share, but these usually got lost in the shuffle. There was brief silence as we gave thanks, then into the turkey, hacked to pieces, but done. Keep in mind my mother's parents were from New England.

There are dozens of web sites covering Thanksgiving disasters.

Lovely story in a fine Pebble Beach home, family and guests at the table, and Mary, the maid, walks in with the turkey on a platter. Turkey slips off the platter, skids across the floor, guests horrified. The hostess, however, says "Mary, you may take this turkey back to the kitchen, and bring in the other one!" Credit this, I think, to Reader's Digest!

There are, of course, after Thanksgiving disasters, like Turkey Soup. My in-laws had a fine tradition, leaving the carcass out on the sink, covered with a damp dishtowel. For two or three days the family nibbled, and on about the fourth day everybody got sick. Couldn't figure it out.

One other cautionary word. It is a well-known fact that sewers tend to back up on Thanksgiving and not sure why, but that can certainly mess up the day. Just a suggestion. Call Roto Rooter the week before Thanksgiving, clean out the drains, just in case. (I say Roto Rooter since I did a commercial for them years ago. Actually, any good plumber will do.)

Last year Susie and I celebrated at Epiphany Church in Marina, serving turkey and ham to a grateful congregation and members of the community. It was a great experience and somebody else did the dishes.

Giving the Thanksgiving prayer, if you are called upon, can be a challenge. It's easy to say too little, or too much. Once you have the attention of the table, however just say, "God, Thank You! (pause, then) Amen!" That says it all, and that's all He wants to hear.

*   *   *   *   *

Time Sensitive

A couple of days ago I heard a wild-eyed congressman shouting at me... If I liked the postal service, I would love the Health Care Plan! (Not sure what to call it.) Wow! Good news! I *love*, or at least admire the post office. OK, so it apparently operates at a loss, but good grief! What about congress! Not taking sides on health care since I don't understand it, but attacks on how we get our mail are unfair and just a touch ignorant.

Members of the House and Senate I think still have franking (pre E-mail) privileges and since that helps keep us informed... Oh Boy... all well and good. But let's see. How about the good old Internet? E-mail from Congress! Free! And no extra strain on the post office!

Back to the good old USPS for a minute. For less than four bits, I drop a letter in the slot, and it ends up at the proper address in a day or two! And there are millions each day. Just think that through. The term "snail mail" does have a certain ring and there have been times when an envelope gets lost, but I've also heard of E-mails winding up in front of the wrong eyes. I know. If you've got nothing to be ashamed of, what difference does it make! Well, that's a pretty broad assumption.

Receiving mail at home, way back in the good old days, an occasional letter addressed to me, in a fine hand and with a touch of perfume, would be waiting for me on the hall table. I knew that unless I got it from the mailman's hand, it would be steamed open, scanned and resealed, by my loving mother. While, of course, she was interested, and curious, she also wanted to make secretly sure that I was not being led in the wrong direction, no matter how sweet was Sally, the correspondent! Well, Sally and her letters are long gone, as is my mother, but remember with me, the pleasure, pain, excitement, and satisfaction of letters, "sealed with a kiss," or not. You knew that he or she had actually *touched* that piece of paper, and *licked* the envelope. Yes, some things are missing in E-mail. Well, you could always plant a kiss on the computer screen.

This brings me to Valentine's Day, which once again, is almost upon us. If you think this is just for kids, I wish you well. It can be a seriously difficult day if for any number of reasons, all sad, you no longer have a sweetheart, but try this. There is some other lonesome soul around and about, and it would be very nice to send along a valentine, signed "secret." It can always be acknowledged later.

Now friends, I know those electronic cards are cute and convenient, and I guess are better than nothing. And yet, there is a magic with the valentine that comes by mail, "snail mail," if you must. I don't want to put dear old Hallmark out of business, and sure, nothing wrong with hearts and flowers with a catchy rhyme.

But just for a minute, remember fifth or sixth grade, and that cute girl or boy who made your heart flutter, and an envelope with a folded scrap of paper, "I Love You." In later years the envelope with the stamp upside down, and maybe a lipstick print.

If you have already bought the card, and along with a dozen roses, plan to present all this with the first glass of wine, it is bound to be a very nice evening. But this year, just take a chance. Even if you and your sweetie share the same E-mail address, trust both me and USPS, write "I Love You, Sweet Valentine," pop it in an envelope with an upside down Forever stamp, and drop it in the box. Up to you, but it could be a lovely afternoon.

* * * * *

Ballet! Not Belly!

As you might recall, I'm nuts about the Smuin Ballet, and flashing back, I don't think we had much exposure to ballet back in the good old days. Later, in The City, I enjoyed The Nutcracker with my kids enough to last a lifetime. I was happy to hear Tony LaRussa had the Oakland A's working out with the local ballet troupe, but that was a long time ago. And speaking of Nutcracker, none of this to detract from the Dance Kids show, coming up! See one, see them both! And not only that, you can get opera Live! now in Monterey, but that's another story.

Memory fades, and there might have been a lot of "culture" on the Monterey Peninsula in the 1940s and 1950s, but Big Bands, Swing, and Jitterbug were more popular than say, Swan Lake. We did have Community Concerts, misprinted once in the Herald as Community Carnage. Only one I can remember is Rose Resnick, and a great lady she was. A blind concert pianist, she spent her life as an activist for the visually impaired.

Now, back to Smuin. I first saw the troupe a couple of years ago, a very lucky accident, and friends, I don't know what it takes to get you there, but let me just say they give a very sensual, sensational performance. I've mentioned this to several friends, and get a yawn or two, and "I'm just not into ballet." Neither was I!

Part of the prejudice is the word, "Ballet," tutus and toes. Some guys might be turned off by "Dancing With The Stars," (I know. It's rigged.) but how about The Dallas Cowboy cheer leaders! Friends, Smuin is better! One of my friends, before he saw Smuin, claimed he wasn't too interested in men in tights. I reminded him of the 49ers, and he modified his opinion. And then, of course, are the lasses, also in tights.

If you are the least bit interested in physical fitness, you will Wow! over these guys and gals! They use their bodies full out, and all this to music! Not an ounce of fat in the entire troupe, the performance is a combination of gymnastics, acrobatics, and as they say in their promo, a "just a little bit naughty, but very nice." According to The Herald earlier this year, they are "Classy and Sassy... a lively mix of classical and cool!" This two hour work out would put the 49ers to shame – oh, never mind – and they don't even break a sweat! These are very special people. An added plus, in the audience are little girls dressed in ballet outfits, in tow with their moms and dads.

"Quick, quick!" you say! "Where, when!" December 3 and 4 at Sunset in Carmel!

If I were rich I'd say "I'll give you your money back if you don't like it," but you'll just have to take my word.

* * * * *

Semper Fry!

Along about lunchtime I flash back to the good old days of good food, and then realize that there's even more good food right now and right here! It doesn't take much to recall those old favorites. Last weekend, celebrating a Cal Poly graduation, my son, Scott, hosted a dinner in San Miguel, of all places, at The Tenth Street Cafe. The big deal here is that 10th Street is a real Basque restaurant, and those are slowly fading from the scene. Of course there aren't as many Basque sheepherders around any more. After weeks in the boondocks taking care of the flocks, they pulled into towns up and down the Central Valley, looking for food straight from the Pyrenees. If you spent any time in Bakersfield you remember Noriega's and The Woolgrowers, still around and busy, even with very few sheepherders. In North Beach in SF we had what I think was the best, The Espana Hotel, across the street from Des Alpes, also a winner, but Espana had the classic long tables, no menus, but you knew what to expect. Lots and lots of food, all family style, starting with a rich, spicy soup, then platters of fish, chicken, lamb chops, with everything else in between. Always a pitcher of good Dago Red on the table, and plenty of bread. Tenth Street is close, dinner only, 7:00 sharp, and plan on two and a half hours before the bread pudding arrives. Although San Miguel is worth the trip, don't over look a good Basque place in San Juan Baptista!

Well, back to Pacific Grove, and Egg Foo Yung at Tom's Cafe, and for a quick snack it was down to Ruby's or Johansen's for the world's best hamburgers. (Why don't root beer floats taste as good as they used to?) And a long, long time ago, abalone at Pop Ernst's. Remember? You could hear the thump thump, thump of abalone being pounded out at the end of the wharf. And Oh, Boy! Those crab pots bubbling away, and you could still catch that great smell way down Alvarado. And that takes me to The First Brick House, where a local family made the world's best tamales.

Always a treat to visit Bernstein's Fish Grotto on Powell in SF, now long gone. The front was the bow of a ship, the sour dough perfect, but our own Fisherman's Wharf had an edge on the chowder. Lot's of out of town icons in the old days. Trader Vic's out on San Pablo, and of course in SF, Ernie's! It was the atmosphere as much as the food, with bordello style decor. That's what I was told, anyway. My Dad's standard line after a good meal on our peninsula, "Boys, you couldn't do any better at Ernie's!"

And speaking of whorehouses, up stairs, so goes the legend, (*way* before Sally Stanford) Jack's on Sacramento possibly had the best food in the City. The Rex Sole, swimming in butter, especially good after a Beefeater/rocks. That was in the old days when we drank at lunch.

But wait, you say! What about all of North Beach! La Pantera, Mario's Bohemian Cigar Store, the Washbag! Just a quick stroll down Columbus and you smelled like garlic for a week! OK, OK! Chinatown! And Sam's Grill and Tadich's! Well, more later, but just tonight, how about a quick bounce into The Mission Ranch, or Rio Grill, or Joe Rombi's or one of John Pisto's places! Bon Appetite!

* * * * *

Sea Fever

Flashing back, there was something in us who grew up on Monterey Bay to want a boat. For those of you who understand, I don't need to explain. To those who don't, it wouldn't make any difference. I guess it starts in the bathtub with the Ivory Soap and the rubber duck. Something wonderful about something that floats. Any body of water would do and once upon a time we lived on the Kern River. My brother, Brooks, and I thought a raft would be a good idea, but luckily it broke up and sank before floating us merrily, merrily, down the stream.

Brooks, who you will remember as Monterey's Harbor Master, worked long and hard, I think in the sixth grade, and hammered together a modest punt. More like a floating box, but it worked, leaked a little, but happily carried Brooks around the pilings at Wharf Number Two. Brooks later became a blue water Captain, sailing around the world and then some, but that's another story.

Around the time that we were in high school, my dad discovered an old wooden life boat hull at a Coast Guard Station up on the Delta. "Sure," they said. "Take it away," and he did. Dad saw promise in this derelict, as he did in many things, also another story, and our garage at 18th and Laurel became our shipyard. As I remember, the boat was about twenty feet, and even though old and tired it had a certain class and shape.

For months we scraped, sanded, polished, and then painted the hull, inside and out, a beautiful high gloss marine white. She had taken on an identity by now, and Dad named her The Marilynn B., after Mom, patient and admiring. Somewhere Dad located an old Frisco Standard 5 horse single cylinder engine in good shape, and a bronze propeller.

Then, the big day! The Launch! A lumber truck hoisted aboard our pride and joy and off we followed in the green Chevy to Fisherman's Wharf! Right next to what now is Abalonetti's was the boat hoist. Up she went, and over the side, down to the water below. Some cheers, maybe a few smiles, but we were ecstatic! Dad, Brooks and I scrambled down the ladder and stepped aboard. And then, Good Grief! The Marilynn B. began to leak! Like a sieve! Brooks and I manned the pumps, put aboard as an after thought, and the old Sicilian sailors, leaning over the rail above, politely reminded Dad that we had neglected to caulk! Happily, they wandered away, with other fish to fry.

The three of us pumped away for an hour or so, the wood swelled, and we were ready for the first and last voyage of the Marilynn B. The Frisco Standard, dependable "one lunger," fired up, and out the harbor we went. Around the bend beyond the canneries to Sino's Boat Yard, dropped anchor and we waded ashore.

Dad had to leave the next morning on the Del Monte Express to make connections in The City. Brooks and I were to paddle the boat… now known as "the boat," around to Sino's ways, bring it up out of the water, let it rest until we could do the caulking thing.

That was the plan. Sad to say, however, the anchor didn't hold, and the next morning "the boat" was rolling back and forth on the granite beach. Brooks and I waded, pushed it out afloat, smashing my big right toe in the effort. Sino pulled the vessel out and it languished in the yard for several years. Dad sold the Frisco Standard and the bronze prop, and a possible buyer of the remains found that a screwdriver slid very easily through the hull. No sale. Well, Brooks went to Cal Maritime, and I wound up in the Navy for a few years, but nothing like the maiden voyage of The Marilynn B!

* * * * *

Good-bye Gertie

Flashing back for those of you who went to Monterey High, 1964 and earlier, you will remember Dean of Girls, Miss Gertrude "Gertie" Rendtorff. This of note since I have owned and lived in the Rendtorff home in Carmel for many years. I'm in the "distribution" mode of my life now, downsizing, and this Carmel treasure will soon be loved and honored by another steward. I proudly describe the house as a "collectible."

Visitors note that it is really "Old Carmel," and has a pedigree increasingly rare in our village by the sea. Professor Karl and Mrs. Rendtorff bought the original three lots from The Carmel Development Company, had Murphy build the house and in they moved in 1913. This section on Camino Real, North of Ocean Ave, was known as Professor's Row and it was only natural that Professor Rendtorff who ran the German department at Stanford take up residence. They moved here permanently in 1929 after he retired.

Gertrude earned her degree and earned a Masters at Stanford and did graduate work at Mills. In 19 and 1931 she taught at Bakersfield Union High School, unaware that around the corner at Mercy Hospital a kid who would eventually own her Carmel home was being born! She arrived at Monterey High in 1932, retiring 1965. Reports are that Gertie was a strict disciplinarian, but also a kind and helpful counselor. Like Mother Teresa with a whip! Voted Woman of the Year in 1964, she died in 1975. She was a beautiful little kid and I have a photo to prove it. For those of you who believe in ghosts, I do feel the spirit of Gertrude from time to time. For those of you who don't, I get inspiration from her pictures and evidence of her presence here, still intact.

Like most homes built almost a hundred years ago, it has suffered some insults, but with careful restoration and updates, the Craftsmen style, with redwood paneling, gives the place a real soul. We treasure some of the original scars, scratches at the bottom of some doors, put there by long gone dachshunds, and other scratches by a window where a long gone cat used to enter. Some decorative carvings still remain, and the booth, once part of an inglenook, is untouched. The Rendtorff spirits sometimes whisper their approval.

When Carmel was more of a village than it is today, bohemians, writers, as well as professors would have visited the Rendtorff home, walked through the oaks and admired Gertrude's pelargoniums. Just down the street, George Sterling and Lincoln Steffans, and up a block on Monte Verde, Robin and Una Jeffers before Tor House. Maybe fifty years from now they'll say "Look! That's where old man Bowhay used to live!"

And one more thing... they don't ring a bell at the bottom of the market!

*   *   *   *   *

Defining Moments...

This may be a little heavier than my usual stuff, but as I flash back on the good old days, before and since, I find myself remembering those "defining moments," after which things were not the same. I think you know what I mean. Any number of things; graduations, weddings, romances, both good and bad, deaths in family and of friends, recognition of accomplishments, even trauma. These punctuations in life may be question marks or exclamations, seldom periods, but maybe a parentheses or two.

I was nudged into these considerations, sitting through a series of events this past week at a very impressive Ivy League commencement and graduation. These were certainly defining moments for the graduates, not to mention the parents whose credit scores possibly got some relief! Regardless of your politics you will appreciate the Class Day remarks by Bill Clinton. Log on to livestream.com/yale. This might even be a defining moment for you!

Graduation from Pacific Grove Grammar School – now Robert H Downs – was a big deal in 1943. No Middle School or Junior High to soften the jolt, and we were very young! The boys all wore blue denim pants and jackets – there was a war on, you know – and I'm sure the girls will remind me of their outfits. This was a defining moment, with lots more to follow. Other graduations, ceremonies, triumphs and tragedies, a combination of scar tissue and polish. A life without regrets is a life not fully lived! Does that make you feel any better?

The current crop of graduates, throughout the country, are told there has never been a better time to face the world! Opportunity, challenge, need, and demands of broken societies and hungry souls. The old story, "To whom much is given, much is required," or something like that. I didn't hear *any* kids worry about a job, career, or future. We can worry for them. I have a hunch, too, that they will do less texting and tweeting as they get out and about, too busy *doing*, teaching, helping, and creating.

A point here, to maybe put your teeth on edge.... Clinton pointed out how many of us read, listen, and talk only to the people with whom we agree, maybe not taking the chance of exposure to a new idea or point of view. He claims that every day he attempts to listen to somebody with whom he disagrees. (Go ahead! Roll your eyes! *I heard that!)* Just kidding!

Well, I guess we can make the point that each day is a defining moment, a new commencement, and yes, I know. We all have one very defining moment down the road!

* * * * *

Drive-Ins!

Since most of us... OK, some of us... grew up in either the front seat or the back seat of a car, easy now to flashback to Drive-In Movies! They were a big time part of our culture and as recently – *recently?* – as the 1950s there were over 200 in California alone. There are now nineteen left in the state. Quite a history, if you want to look it up. There were two or three in Monterey County, now bulldozed and turned into shopping centers and apartment complexes. Some of the old locations are now flea markets, parking lots, or drag racing sites.

But Oh, what a thrill on those summer nights to pile into the car, some kids hiding in the trunk or in the back seat, and zip to The Drive-In! Under the massive screen or the projection booth, there was popcorn, hot dogs, cokes, and candy bars, and anything else to build the profit. You could stumble through the dark, sneak a peek into some of the cars on the way to the rest room, but there were plenty of lighted intermissions with lovely ushers guiding customers to the snack bar. Some theaters featured play areas for the kiddies while parents snuggled in the car.

And speaking of snuggling... some Drive-Ins – actually, all of them – were known as "passion pits," and I'm told, well deserved. Inexpensive, private and comfortable, often with romantic mood set on the screen, volume on the speaker hanging inside the driver side window turned down low. In the good old days the front seats were bench style, not like modern bucket seats that may not cancel physical contact, but do require a certain amount of determination. Yes, I know. There was then, and now, the back seat. The gear shift, always an inconvenience, but if pushed forward, and to right in the rear drive position, not much of a problem.

Great stories and memories when we sometimes felt part of the story on the screen. I'm told of either romantic or cliff hanger scenes when the gal caught up in the drama, either scooting forward, or slumping down, oblivious to her date's right hand, later claiming she knew exactly what was going on!

Coming up for air at intermission, time for a snack and a drink. A cute little blonde said she would really like some cotton candy. Well, back it came and she almost squealed in delight, however, at first lick she sneezed and pink goo covered the window, dashboard and floor mats. I understand her face was sticky, too. Next day, Dad asked what was *that* all about!

As you know, Drive-Ins and drive-thrus are not to be confused, although some times one led to the other. Story is the first drive through in California was the innovation of our friend, In-N-Out back in the late 1930s, and although I understand the convenience issue, foods of various descriptions can certainly mess up a car. Same with those happy drive-in restaurants, the cute car hops scooting up on roller skates to take your order. A French fry under the seat lasts forever.

Well, progress will not be denied. I understand the Drive-In movies are still fun, if you can find them. But I think if I was still in the driver's seat I'd suggest a movie on my lap top, parked near The Point, and a taco at Pepper's... later.

* * * * *

Crowning Glory

A few weeks ago I commented on the benefit of sitting in the back of the church. Good place to observe and study ladies hair situations. My story was scholarly and not unkind, but I have been urged, in a spirit of fairness, to say a little something about hair on the heads of gents.

I must say first, that a woman's hair is usually a thing of beauty, or at least, so intended, often a statement of self-esteem, or otherwise. Men generally – I think – don't want to look "different." which is unfortunate since no matter how many hats we wear, our hair can be a nuisance. There are those, too, usually younger, who say "The heck with it! I'll wear a Mohawk or bright green if I want to!" And Ah! The comb over! Ingenious engineering, not only accepted, but admired!

In our early years moms plastered us down with "stickum." In Bakersfield a long time ago, MGM, looking for a kid to play Jody in "The Yearling," herded thousands of us into the ballroom of the El Tejon Hotel. Moms were told to not even *comb* our hair, but plastered I was, and of course, didn't get the part. Oddly enough, Ted Richmond, a later classmate in PG, had his moment of glory with tousled hair, and was slated to be Jody. Sadly, so the story goes, the deer died, and the movie was postponed until Ted was too old for the part. Ted, however, turned out just fine.

Looking back on high school, we loaded our hair with with Vitalis, Brylcream, or pomade (grease) carefully combed, the front pushed into a pompadour, hoping to be mistaken for a movie star. You know, like Elvis or Johnny Cash in later years. I look with some embarrassment at my senior picture. The guys with plenty of hair and plenty of grease wore pompadours in front and Duck Tail (Duck's Butt, with thanks to Disney) in the back. Worthy to mention, when a gal in passionate admiration ran her fingers though her boy friend's hair had to excuse herself to wash her hands... unless, of course, the passion was extreme.

The natural reaction to all this was the crew cut, borrowed from the military.

And sideburns? Still in style, but usually with a "pencil thin mustache," like Boston Blackie, Clark Gable. Vincent Price, or Salvatore Dali. (Speaking of Dali, a long time ago, front row of the old Golden Bough, Macbeth on stage, some honey on my left, Salvatore Dali on my right! Short on conversation.)

Well not for me to talk about facial hair. Makes me itch, but I'm told that a little fuzz, over the lip, or under the chin, has been know to attract the ladies.

Good news that as we gents became seriously mature, the hairstyles are now happily casual, loose, with just a little light spray, not enough to discourage passionate admiration. A nice full head of white or light grey signals a certain amount of experience and self-assurance. OK, so Grecian Formula might slow down the process, the inevitable, but sooner or later.... I confess a certain curiosity about the very shiny heads, now popular on all ages. Yul Brynner set the trend, tough on barbers, and I wonder now how the elected hairless keep their scalps in such perfect condition. Never mind. It's not important. Well, in any case, hooray for hats.

I'll close, with the bald Indian who wore a teepee to keep his wigwam.... Get it?

Toupee? Wig Warm?

* * * * *

Some Books Smell Better Than Others

Flashing back, I grew up in Pacific Grove, which is somewhat low and damp, and went away to college in Albuquerque, New Mexico, which is high and dry. As much as I loved the Land of Enchantment, there was something missing, like Pacific Grove water, which you could almost chew. But coming back for Christmas, I walked in the front door, took a deep breath, and knew I was home. There was that deep, musty smell of years of damp, and mold. It was up the stairs where panels of Masonite had been less than completely dry for years, in my bedroom, the kitchen cooler, and the point of all this, in the basement, with boxes of books! There were *National Geos, Reader's Digests*, encyclopedias, *Weekly Readers*, and best sellers from New England before the Westward tilt. Well, that's just the way it was.

Now wait! The reason for all this is the Friends of the Carmel Library Book Sale, which is one really big deal! Not until August, and you can only imagine the quality of the books offered, and the prices way below which you could get on Groupon. (You could look it up.) Dealers sneak in from all over the state, grab up these bargains, and get modestly rich on resale! You can too! Or read!

However, buyers of some picky refinement, might well be turned off, or turned away, in the presence of 100 thousand books, if the whole joint – OK, Hall at the Mission – smelled mold or musty. Possibly people from Barstow. The volunteers who box these donated books for sale, are smell sensitive, and one in particular, is known as The Nose! Volumes rank or rotten go into the recycle bin and are recycled as Masonite! Or maybe book covers!

We bring this up since there is a certain protocol in storing books. This may be too late for that copy of *Forever Amber*, now home to sow bugs, but it might come in handy in the store room with Tom Friedman's latest. Down there by the paint cans by that stack of yearbooks, which possibly smelled when they were new. Keep them dry, friends, and away from spiders. A light dusting now and then not a bad idea. On the other hand, before the mold sets in, why not stack them in the front hall, as a reminder to give them away early rather than later! Friends of The Carmel Library have been known to cheer when people drive up to Sunset Center on Tuesday mornings between 10 and noon, with books saved from the cellar! Just so you know, books not sold, are given to other libraries, schools, and nonprofits. I know, I know! For the record, there are a lot of great book sales, and every one good! I don't know if they will accept your used Kindle, but maybe!

* * * * *

The Power of No!

Looking back on the good old days I don't remember the very first time I experienced rejection, but I can sure remember lots of it along the way. I talk about this to reassure you that you are not the only soul to be told "No!" Being told in First Grade that "No, you could not be excused to go to the bathroom" doesn't count. Maybe like in High School you wanted to borrow five bucks, the answer was "No!"

As a young stockbroker, trying to build a client base with cold calls, sometimes the answer was just a click as they hung up. A firm "No!" might have opened the conversation, but "No!" usually meant just that. (Be kind to your telemarketer.)

Now on the tail end of Reunion season, we're reminded of the "No!" we heard in those tender teenage years. Charles' McCabe's mother told him, "Always expect the worst. You'll never be disappointed!," which, of course made the occasional "Yes!" even more satisfying.

Back in the 1940s, Forest Pool up near Boulder Creek, was the teen Mecca in our part of the world. Set in the redwoods, a pool, of course, but also a dance floor, juke box music, and Japanese lanterns. Kids flocked there, up from the beach, summer camp, or family vacation cabins. Three or four of us hopefuls from PG arrived one balmy summer evening, filled with hope and promise. Across the dance floor, like every other dance floor in the world, there was a line of bobby-soxers, also filled with hope, pretending to be bored. Remember? Well, there I stood, hair slicked back, Levis with two inches of turned up cuff, and my Red and Gold letter sweater. I focused on a cute little blonde honey, bit the bullet, strolled up, Stan Kenton doing "Tampico," and I said, simply, "Would you like to dance?" I don't think she even looked at me, and just loud enough for the other girls lined up to hear, "No." Not "Thanks, no," or what I could kiss, or anything like that, just a flat "No!" I wonder if she ever married.

You can tell this left a mark on my self-esteem. And just a year or two earlier, in the family Chevy, I took a pretty little brunette to a movie in Carmel. Maybe a soda afterwards, then up the steps to the front door – I can show you the house on Lincoln – and then a blunder that stayed with me for years... "Heather," I said, her name was Heather, "Can I kiss you?" You guessed it! "No!" I never saw her again. Now, Heather, if you happen to read this, "Too late, too late!" No, No, a thousand times No!

Best No story, PG fiftieth class reunion, class mate asked the gal, even better looking now than then, "Would you like to dance?"

"No," she said. "You wouldn't ask me to dance fifty years ago, and I won't dance with you now." Said sweetly, with a cute smile, but a very satisfying "get even." By the way, the guy wasn't me.

One last. A fraternity brother in college, very short on suave, dated a Theta, finally got up the nerve to ask her, "Ah, would you like to, you know, do it?"

Instead of "No," she said "Of course not!" Then, after an awkward pause, "Well, maybe."

* * * * *

Praise the Aged!

Back in the good old days, the 30s, 40s, and even the 50s, there seemed to be a lot more old people around. My dad, for instance, said that Pacific Grove was the old lady capital of the world. Said they came here to die, but never did! I will say that we took all this for granted. At Mayflower Congregational Church, they were *really* old. Average age probably sixty!

I think it was from these seriously mature ladies and gentlemen that we learned civility and a certain level of good manners. Then, of course, the *knowledge* they were willing to share, and the *experiences*, sea stories, close escapes, not to mention the peril of crossing The Sierra, and sailing around The Horn! And these stories were indeed, really true! My grandmother, as I have told you, was born in a covered wagon. Grandma Bowhay long gone, but the wagon is still in a Hanford museum. She told stories of gun battles, bandits and other perils, not unlike some local conditions, but that's not the point. First grade, one schoolhouse, in the San Joaquin, almost 150 years ago. Rough older kids took delight in terrorizing teachers, running them out of town. Along came Mr. Perkins, the kids all nervous, waiting to see what the big boys would do.

As Mr. Perkins entered the classroom, back by the potbellied stove, he drew a circle about a foot across, on the wall. He strode up to the front, looked at the students, took a six gun out of a leather case, fired six shots over the heads of the students, all shots well inside the circle on the board. He then announced, through the gun smoke, that there would be ORDER in his classroom. There was, indeed, and later he was superintendent of schools in Fresno County. You could look it up!

The Forest Hill Hotel was a treasure trove of older people, some mildly eccentric, but all well mannered and nice, especially to young bellhops. In addition to nickels, dimes and quarters, they shared peppermints and sometimes lemon drops. The gentlemen wore vests with watch fobs and almost never went out without a hat. They spoke of lighting rods, buggy whips, chamber pots, garters and prohibition. Hats and gloves for the ladies, and in the privacy of the elevator they would sometimes powder puff their cheeks. In the lobby, brass spittoons, used with great discretion.

They all seemed pleased that they had lived so long, and wanted to be sure that we knew they had once been young, with stories and pictures to prove the point.

Well here we are now, and these todays are pretty darned good, too.

The dramatic increase in life expectancy should, but doesn't produce more old people.

I won't get started on the several treatments and surgeries that postpone oldness. Too much concern about the deficit and all that stuff our grandkids will cope with might well furrow the brow, but it seems to me *our* grandparents also worried about us!

Now we all know that *old* is a state of mind, as well as worn out parts, and of course, *old* is somebody born earlier that you. And too, have you noticed that some old people have *relationships?* Yep, and then some! Those of us who have stretched out the rubber band of life, just love that poetic line, "Come, grow old with me. The best is yet to be."

You'll notice I haven't once said "senior citizen" or "God's waiting room." I mean, after all, I'm only eighty!

• • • • •

Pacific Grove, by Golly!

Flashing back to my hometown, Pacific Grove, I usually don't include those "new" sections, way up the hill or deep in the woods. All fine and nice, but I never delivered papers there, and just don't relate. I walked around downtown yesterday, and although there are changes, both plus and minus, it felt comfortable, calm, and hometown-ish.

One of my treasures is a booklet, compliments of the Board of City Trustees, printed, I think, over a hundred years ago. It describes, in flowery prose, Pacific Grove, California, The Ideal Family Summer and Winter Resort. That PG be developed as a resort was the original intent, and here we are! No saloons, as they promised, and sure, we can buy and drink all we want today, but I don't think there is a real saloon in town. Maybe I don't get out enough. I am pleased to recall that "Pacific" still means peaceful, and the only threats of mayhem are out of sight of children in the Council Chambers.

While downtown is slightly quiet, there is a spirit of confidence, newer and older enterprises that say "we have faith in our hometown." Look at Joe Rombi, adding to one of the best restaurants in the county, and doing great business! And across Lighthouse, waiting in line at The Red House, is worth it. On Seventeenth, you can't overlook Fandango. We grew up just a block away, Eighteenth and Laurel, and what a nice stroll over to Mrs. Filcher's house, now a perfect restaurant. Mom's favorite!

Back in the good old days I can remember at least three grocery stores, and maybe a couple more. There was Friendly Market, Top Hat, Central, and even one in Holman's basement, all in the middle of town, and all busy. What a treat to hear Bill Hellam imitate a trombone as he wrapped a package and snapped the string!

Home food storage was a little tight back in the thirties and earlier, and people shopped at least two or three times a week. Walked! Plenty of business for the grocers. Couldn't freeze much above the ice trays in the Fridge. The "coolers" worked fine, just barely, but along with Union Ice, food kept for a couple of days, then back to the market. Not counting those up on the hill, there's the one and only, Grove Market in the Quonset building on Forest! Charlie Higuera grew up in the grocery business and will show you a picture of his dad behind the counter in his New Monterey store back in the early thirties. Charlie and his partners took a deep breath in 1969, went into debt and took over the slightly ragged Purity Market. What a great thing for PG, and Charlie, in his apron and cap, still runs the show. Friends, this is a hometown operation, and you feel it when you walk in the door. His associates are friendly, happy, and helpful, proud to be a real part of the organization, and boy, what food! Best produce, meat, and deli, and you know it's top of the line. You don't have to be beautiful to work there, but you wouldn't know it, looking around! Charlie's granddaughter, Kristi, mother of twins, and a checker, proves the point!

For a more recent example of faith in the future of Pacific Grove, take a look at the corner of Laurel and Grand! Mary Norton opened nine years ago what is probably the best puzzle gallery west of the Rockies. We're talking here, mostly, about the jigsaw variety, but it doesn't stop there. There are all kinds, shapes, sizes, and colors, and if you can't find one you like, Mary will custom make your own. The cozy atmosphere in I'm Puzzled is like a step back in time. You may feel like you've been there before, and you want to come back. Mary's associate, Yvonne, born and raised in PG, compliments the hometown feeling. And speaking of hometown, Chad, Mary's husband, says "Last Hometown" is OK, but "The Best Hometown!" is better. Sounds good to me.

* * * * *

Pre-Judge... or Prejudice

Just for the record, I've never met a Muslim I didn't like. Matter of fact, I've never met a Muslim. This is not a fair comparison, but I must confess (Catholic word,) that I've run into two or three Protestants that I wasn't sure of.

Lets face it. We all grew up with a lot of prejudice, all depending on State of The Nation, war, peace, economy, or what we heard around the dinner table. The prejudice always seems directed at the whole bunch of the other guys, but individually, we might like them. My dad was the perfect example, admitting that he was deeply prejudiced, different groups and different times. But, for instance, he liked every African American he ever met. Claimed they were Puerto Ricans. He had a brief problem with Jackie Robinson, said he was a communist, visited Russia, and all that. No, no, Dad! That was Paul Robeson! Oh. Dad was wrong about all that, too, but if he'd met him, he would have liked him.

It seems to be part of the human race to be against something, especially those and them. Reasonable and natural, to hate the enemy in war, and I don't have to point all that out.

The them and those have included the Irish, Poles, Chinese, Germans, Japanese, and a lot more in between. And don't forget the Native Americans!

All this not to be confused with school spirit! At Pacific Grove High School we had a difficult time liking the gang from Monterey High. It had nothing to do with Sicilians, Genovese, or Catalan. Let's face it! They were better than us at football! Of course we were better at basketball. And those Carmel Padres! Stuck up? Well, they could run faster than us – some of the time. But individually we later liked and laughed with guys named Sal, or girls named Maria or Heather, regardless where from.

It bothers me to write this, but truth, etc. My mother would say in hushed tones, "Well, we like them very much, they are lovely people, but after all, they are Catholic." Or "She's a lovely girl, nice manners, and very bright, and what a shame... her parents are divorced." All this from a family with six dissolutions, at last count! And no Catholics! Well, a few Episcopalians, but after all!

Time now to refer us back to "South Pacific" and read the lyrics to "You have to be carefully taught...." You can get it on the Internet.

Interesting now, and I suppose always, those folks that never paid much attention to their own religious faith and practice, rise up in righteous invective against people who worship from a different slant. I haven't read The Constitution lately, but I remember something in there that might apply.

Now I can stretch this out, or shorten it, but for goodness sake... one more time, for Goodness sake, hate if you must, especially if it makes you feel better, but consider the possibility that if you do, you might betray a little insecurity in your own skin.

. . . . .

Sing Along With Me

"You Keep Coming Back, Like a Song!" and doesn't it almost drive you nuts when you realize you've been humming Jingle Bells all day long, and here it is February. But these songs, these tunes, these melodies are in our brains, our hearts and souls. Some of them we didn't even like.

Try "If I Knew You Were Coming I'd Have Baked a Cake."

On the other side do you remember a certain song, either your own favorite, or the one you both called "Our Song?"

Eight years old, in my bed on a hot Bakersfield night, across the street a small Drive-In with a jukebox, and I first heard "Star Dust," and I knew then that a better song would never be written. And it still hasn't. "Deep Purple" was close. Anything that Patsy Cline did would almost pull your heart into your throat, but maybe that's just old "Sentimental Me."

Just for fun, dig into that pile of 78s in the basement. So you don't have a turntable? That's OK. Just look at the titles and remember those magical nights at the Scout Hall when some of your records were borrowed, your name taped on.

If you really want to go back to the good old days (just remember that someday, these will be the good old days) sit down at your computer and be amazed that many of the good old tunes are at your fingertips, free! Sure, you know about I Tunes, but don't stop there. Try the jukebox on Tropicalglenn.com, or pick a tune, like "String of Pearls" and you'll wind up with Glenn Miller Radio. Then get on the phone, hum a few bars to that gal that used to live down the street, or maybe that honey in the next room, let her know you can still dance at the Scout Hall! Now they call it Chatauqua, but the place still smells the same, sweat and cologne! Don't even need dance wax any more!

We had plenty of help to pick our favorites. Remember Peter Potter and his Juke Box Jury? If we didn't like the song, he'd smash the platter right on air! Something we'd like to do today with some of the stuff we hear. The best forum of all, I think, was The Lucky Strike Hit Parade!, playing the hits from the mid thirties to the mid fifties, and then off and on in various formats into the seventies. If we dig around enough we might find an old transcription and get Ed Dickinson to play it. Story goes that Snooky Lanson trying for several weeks to do Hound Dog finally hastened the demise of the show, but Lucky Strike lived on! And Lucky Strike Green did go to war! Well, enough.

"So long, for awhile. That's all our songs for a while, So long to your Hit Parade, and the songs that you picked to be played. So Long!"

Go ahead. Hum a few bars, just for fun!

* * * * *

Cool, Clear Water

Memory is a flawed reference, but I'll bet if you suffered from Valley heat in the 1930s and lived anywhere between Mcfarland and Earlimart, you will remember The Delano Plunge. Built, owned and operated by my grandfather, "Dad" Bowhay, a couple of miles south of town, this cool, clear water was about as close to a spa you could get in the San Joaquin. It was built up above ground with miscellaneous rubble, old sidewalk pieces, rocks and bricks, and lined with a solid coat of cement. Deep enough at one end for a diving board, and shallow enough at the other for little kids. The water was disinfected with "blue stone," whatever that was. My brother, Brooks, and I looked longingly at the water and the lucky kids swimming, but our parents fear of polio kept us dry. We did, however, get to paddle around the classy pool at the Buckingham ranch near Mcfarland and later learned to swim in the river behind Kernville, but that's another story.

I think admittance to the plunge was a nickel or a dime, but not much more. You remember there were a few poor kids up and down the Valley, and Dad Bowhay always looked the other way if they snuck in for a dip. While we watched, Granddad opened bottles of Nehi Root Beer and poured it in cups with Wayne's ice cream, and passed some of that along to the visiting kids, too.

The other big deal on the Bowhay Ranch was the menagerie, which was close to being a small zoo. Granddad had always had pets and liked animals, and creatures by the dozens showed up and stayed. Some were old and tired, and he nursed them back, and some were gifts from friends. In addition to horses, sheep, and cows and deer there were porcupines, a cheetah, a bobcat, badgers, desert tortoises, an eagle, a monkey, and an ostrich!

The monkey, Jocko, bit me on my arm and the scar finally faded, but wow! What a trophy! A real monkey bite! But that was nothing compared to riding on the back of the ostrich!

And of course, the birds, all fluttering around loose. All kinds of pheasants and chickens, laying eggs at random around the ranch, and the world's noisiest creatures, the peacocks! The best thing about peacocks, other than the feathers, was that they roasted beautifully and tasted better than turkey.

Well, sweet memories, my brother and I, along with the sheep dog, Old Tejon, trudging around the ranch with Granddad, peeing behind the berry bushes, then into Grandma's kitchen for sugar cookies and milk still warm from the cow.

The Bowhay ranch long gone, and most of the Bowhays, but tell me, friends, is The Valley still a little bit the same? If not, that's why I write to you!

* * * * *